Awakened Souls

AWAKENED SOULS

COURTNEY BECK

Copyright © 2019 by Courtney Beck
All rights reserved. This book or any portion thereof may not be reproduced or used in any manner whatsoever without the express written permission of the author except for the use of brief quotations in a book review.

Courtney Beck
www.courtneybeck.co
courtney@courtneybeck.co

For my wife Jules, the love of my life and the one who helps me walk this path, sometimes with a gentle nudge and sometimes with a loving shove.

And for my friend Ariella, a bright star in what can be a dark sky. Your impact on my life will not be forgotten.

Contents

1. The Path to Enlightenment 1
2. Transitions 7
3. Glory 12
4. Trust 17
5. Sacredness 20
6. Shedding 23
7. Meditation 28
8. Magnitude 35
9. Sanity 39
10. Light 43
11. Talking 47
12. Magic 50
13. Hope 53
14. Speed 57
15. Belief 60
16. Patience 64
17. Concentration 67
18. Destiny 70

19. Mastery 73

20. Money 77

21. Fears 80

22. Marvelling 83

23. Roads 86

24. Travel 90

25. Challenges 92

26. Guidance 95

27. Longevity 98

28. Ego 101

29. Molecules 106

30. Expectations 109

31. Grandeur 112

32. Clarity 115

33. Neglect 118

34. Bravery 121

35. Change 124

36. Divine Intervention 128

37. Mastery of Self 132

38. Letting Go 135

39. Promises 140

40. Money: Part 2 144

41. Channeling 147

42. Managing Your Time 150
43. Home 154
44. Progress 158
45. Momentum 161
46. Commitment 164
47. Maintaining the Body and Mind 168
48. Health 171
49. Hope: Part 2 174
50. Electricity 177
51. Fear and Ego 180
52. Movement 184
53. Friendship 187
54. Transient Beings 190
55. Lifestyle 193
56. Harmony 197
57. Magic 201
58. Luck 204
59. Freedom 207
60. Gains and Losses 210
61. Cherish 213
62. Misfortune 216
63. Fears 218
64. Interruptions 222

65. Your Unspeakable Truth 224

66. Courage 227

67. Madness 231

68. Being Open 234

69. Masks 237

70. Entry Points 240

71. Energy 243

72. Pathways 246

73. Light 249

74. Rigidity 252

75. Replenishment 255

76. Longevity: Part 2 258

77. Waterfalls 261

78. Chains 263

79. Willingness 266

80. Progress 269

81. Enlightenment 272

82. Magnificence 276

83. Transformation 279

84. Intrusions 282

85. Faith VS Belief 285

86. The Sky 289

87. Courage: Part 2 295

88. Circling Back 298

89. Regeneration 302

90. Masterpieces 306

91. Energy: Part 2 309

92. Energy and Meditation 312

93. Transcendance 315

94. Energy Exchanges 318

95. Emptiness 321

96. Leaving the Path 324

97. Holiness 328

98. Peace 331

99. Chemistry 333

100. Commitment 336

101. Anonymity 339

102. Wholeness 341

103. Investments 344

104. Hope: Part 3 346

105. Work 348

106. Bursts of Energy 350

107. Destiny 353

108. Abandoning the Path 356

109. Interests 360

110. Redemption 363

111. Missteps 367
112. Elegance 370
113. Frugality 373
114. Wisdom 377
115. Agony 382
116. Symbols 385
117. Arrival 389
118. Resistance 393
119. Freedom 397
120. Traffic 402
121. The Will to Live 406
122. Sacrifice 413
123. Nature 418
124. Custodians 421
125. Christmas 424
126. Elasticity 427
127. Celebration 431
128. Vision 435
129. Mental Stress 439
130. Coma 443
131. Greed 447
132. Destiny: Part 2 450
133. The Body 454

134. Children 457

135. Antidote 460

136. Abilities 463

137. Flight 468

138. Choices 472

139. The End 477

For Those Who Have Woken 483

1

THE PATH TO ENLIGHTENMENT

This book will help you to look deep within yourself. Like the ocean, the water begins in blue and ends in black. You must be prepared to swim through both to find what lies at the bottom. If you are brave enough to keep swimming, you will find what you are seeking.

The path to enlightenment is unlike any other. It is the pilgrimage of those seeking to re-commune with the divine. The path to enlightenment is what we are all unconsciously seeking, but it is only those who consciously seek that will find it.

To become enlightened, we must abandon all attachment to the body and human things on Earth. While we may have love, we must be able to let love go for our soul to ascend beyond who and what we are now. The path to enlightenment is not an easy path, which is why so many do not accomplish it. Only the true seekers and those with the determination and grit of a million people will find the pearl of our existence.

We must be prepared to face the ugliest parts of our humanity and our inner darkness. It is only through venturing into the forest of our darkness that we will begin to see the light. It is only through facing our greatest fears that we may find ourselves stripped back enough to know who we are truly are and who we may become.

The Earth is a simulation, and it is there to exist as a living classroom. You need not chase down your fears to face them, as on Earth, we deliver you your fears daily. You will never know which fears you will need to face, or which fears you had signed up to overcome when you were a soul in the sky.

Every life on Earth is here with a purpose that your soul signed a contract for in the sky. You knew your journey here before you arrived. You knew the trials and tribulations you would need to go through to find enlightenment, and despite these perceived challenges, your soul still agreed to come here. Earth is the most challenging classroom we have in our existence. After you ascend and become enlightened, there are other classrooms you may attend, but there is only one Earth.

Earth is unique because you are disconnected from the source and all of her information on your arrival. On Earth, you have a physical body, allowing you to feel physical, mental, and emotional pain that is inescapable. The only way to succeed on Earth is not to acquire earthly things, but to embrace the pain and joy of life on Earth and to swim through it like a swan swims gracefully on a lake. There will be some days where you will feel like a swan drowning underneath a waterfall, and other days where you will glide through your lessons like a swan glides across a calm lake. You will experience both.

Life on Earth means death to the ego. Once on Earth, you are no longer protected from the lessons you have asked to be taught. Life on Earth means there is no escape until death frees you from this beautiful but painful existence.

The faster you learn your lessons, the sooner you will reach the enlightened state. What you must keep in mind is that there are three levels of consciousness here on Earth.

The first level is human. On the human level, you are seeking to establish yourself on Earth. You are learning to make your way as a former spirit and newly formed human being. You may experience this for many lifetimes. To leave this level, you must realize that life on Earth is an illusion and a school of our creation.

Level two is coming to know and understand your spirit, free of religion. This level is recognizing you are more than a human being. You are a spirit. In level two, you will realize you have human abilities, and also have spiritual abilities. To leave this level, you must know and understand the potential of both, incorporating both into your life.

Level two is realizing you are more than human, but recognizing you are currently residing within a human body. It is using the body you have been given to accomplish tasks on Earth on behalf of the masters.

Level three is your ascension back to the sky and back to the stars. Your human body, while it is still there is just a vessel for you to accomplish your goals here on Earth. You are no longer driven or affected by human things. More than your body, you are a spirit. This is the level where your spirit surpasses the body. This is the stage where you will feel most alone as many will not understand your desire to pull back from life, to abandon possessions and the race called 'Life.'

This book is for those who are currently on levels two and three.

If you are reading this book and what I have said resonates with you, then you are ready to begin. The writing and teachings you will read here will test your mind, body, heart, and soul. What you must remember is that what you knew in the sky is no longer, and you must re-learn how your fate will ultimately bring you back to the sky. It is only by moving through our fears and our greatest tests that we will see ourselves for who we are. The body is just a body. The mind is just a mind, made for your earthly existence. The soul is your spirit, and your spirit has lived for eternity.

To ascend and become enlightened once again, you must realize that the mind does not matter, the body is the way you experience the world, and your soul is the being that Earth is longing to reveal.

If you can show your soul to yourself and others on Earth, you will find enlightenment. You will not find your soul in others; you will not find it in things, wealth, or knowledge. Your soul is hidden inside you, like buried treasure waiting to be unearthed.

This book will help you to look deep within yourself. Like the ocean, the water begins in blue and ends in black. You must be prepared to swim through both to find what lies at the bottom. If you are brave enough to keep swimming, you will find what you are seeking.

2

TRANSITIONS

If what you want is to move from level one to levels two and three, then you must be happy to lose all that you have collected in order to find what you have lost, yourself.

When we move between levels, we need to transition.

Transitioning between levels is much like a snake losing its skin or a butterfly turning into a moth.

When we are in level one, we are butterflies. The more accomplished we see ourselves to be, the brighter the color of our wings. It is when we realize that being a butterfly no longer makes us happy that we must transition back into the moth before we can transform again. In our lives, we must seek to be butterflies within, not out.

Like the dance of the lyrebird, being in level one is about feeling success, accomplishment, and finding a mate. Level one is about collecting 'things' and showing what we have found.

When we realize that things no longer make us happy, we must be willing to shed our beautiful colors and become dull again so that we may understand that colors do not make the butterfly, it is the structure and the being that makes a butterfly a butterfly. When we see a white butterfly, we still call it a butterfly. To discover who we are, we must realize that even as a stripped back version of ourselves, our form and our being does not change.

Fewer adornments do not strip us of our being; they mean fewer distractions. By wearing less, we allow people to see who we truly are, without color.

In between transitions, we may feel like we become the moth. We may lose interest in things, people, and places we previously loved. We may feel dull, lost, and listless. What we must realize is that to become who we are, we must first realize who we are not. When we can realize who we are not, we can then work on becoming who we were born to be. Not what the world wants us to be, but the purest version of ourselves.

If we look at the sea, what lies beneath the sea is the seabed. We never see the seabed, yet it is the foundation of the ocean. When we see the ocean, we only see the beautiful blues and greys of the water. We only want to see the beautiful blues and greys. To know, understand, and embrace the ocean, we must know the seabed and the sea itself. Both are interconnected, and the ocean is not one without the other.

On the path to enlightenment, we must be prepared to lose the brightness of our wings to see the wing itself.

We must be ready to drop the version of ourselves we have created, to know there are no versions, only the true self, covered up with who we believe the world wants us to be. What if we told you there was no world, and this is the illusion? To move through the illusion, you must realize that your curated self- does not matter. Your true self-holds the key to all of your happiness, hopes, and dreams.

The self you are trying to be by fitting in here on Earth is an illusion you are creating. To become who you truly are, you must realize there is no value in being the lyrebird. To find enlightenment, be happy to be the bird that is grey and can move unseen.

If what you want is to move from level one to levels two and three, then you must be happy to lose all that you have collected to find what you have lost, yourself.

When you find your true self, you will realize those material things never mattered. They were just distractions on the road to nowhere — a house of mirrors at a fair. When you are comfortable to look at yourself in the mirror, free of colors and distractions, you have transitioned from level one to level two. In level two, what we wish for you to see when you look in the mirror is beyond yourself to the limitless spirit that you are.

The path to enlightenment is not about how much you can collect, or the price you can pay for happiness. It is about finding happiness and peace within. It is feeling comfortable in both stillness and pain, at the bottom of the ocean and the top, on stormy days and in the sunshine.

The seabed never moves; it only shifts over time. Look deeply within, at the seafloor of your soul, and you will see yourself distilled. Look only at the top of the ocean, and you will see a beauty that changes with the days and minutes.

If you wish to seek enlightenment, you must sacrifice the masks you wear and show your real face, heart, and mind. The path back to ourselves is not as smooth as tearing off the masks we have worn for so many years. It is much like losing an extension of ourselves. To be who we are, we must be happy to see ourselves naked and show ourselves in our most naked form to others. To become enlightened, we must realize that we don't exist, and the elaborate games we play are just that, games. To realize who you are, you must understand all that you are not. To realize all that you are not is to realize the potential of what you may become, not as a human being, but as a spirit.

3

GLORY

Do not strive for glory on Earth, strive for oneness. When we are one, we recognise we are equal to all others.

On Earth, we assimilate glory with our path and assume it means success in conquering life. We should not aim to conquer life; we should seek to become one with it, to merge ourselves so entirely with it that one cannot tell where one ends, and the other begins.

When we come to Earth, we agree to fulfill our purpose here. We agree to bring all we were in the sky so that we may bring some of the sky to Earth. Because in the sky, we have not experienced a physical body or lived a life with 'things.' When we come to Earth, and our memories have been wiped clean, we do not remember that in the sky, we had nothing and we were happy with that.

When we arrive on Earth, we are amazed at Earth's beauty, and we are excited at the prospect of living here. As babies, we appreciate the world for the purity and potential it holds for us. As we grow into adults, we become swept up in accumulating all that we can on Earth, believing that success equates to ownership. It does not.

We perceive glory on Earth to be winning against and above all others who reside here. How far we have strayed from our predetermined paths.

Glory on Earth and glory in the sky mean two very different things. Now you know what glory means on Earth, would you like to know what glory means to us?

In the sky, glory is the clear connection we have with the source and to each other. Glory is the relationship we have where there is no difference between us and another, as we are all the same. When we are all the same, we are no longer able to tell where one spirit begins, and another ends as there is only oneness.

On Earth, you are all trying to make your way separately or in small groups. If only you realized the potential of operating as a whole, all of humanity working to the one purpose of peace and harmony. Imagine what you could achieve if all individuals were moving together towards this single goal. There would be no fear, as for how can there be fear when there is oneness?

Fear is an emotion that segregates and separates. It separates those in groups into those acting on their own and those in groups to being separated from the wider whole. When we see ourselves above another, we are not above them; we are showing the world we are below them.

The only antidote to fear is learning to understand each other, the Earth and all of her creatures. When we understand all that is and our place within it, we can no longer feel fear as fear has nothing to feed on.

What we must realize is that glory on Earth relies on you as one individual conquering and taking from another. Conquering another is not glory; it is pain. Perhaps not pain for you now, but pain for you in the future as your soul bears the weight of taking from those who cannot give.

Do not strive for glory on Earth; strive for oneness.

When we are one, we recognize we are equal to all others, and we understand our highest potential lies in working together. When we are one, we realize that glory on Earth is about the self and not the whole. Take glory and exchange it for understanding.

The moment we can put our fear and ego aside and blend ourselves into all that surrounds us is the moment we will feel peace. When we can accept we are all the same, no one smarter or more valuable than another is when you will feel our love.

If we are to overcome our selfishness on Earth, we must show love to all human beings, plants, and animals. Love is not rational and does not divide; love is what makes us whole and what keeps us open to what could be. Love is acceptance. Love holds no bounds, and love does not doubt the worthiness of another. Therefore, as we begin a movement towards oneness, we ask you first act with love. Love is easy to understand and easy to begin. Treat all who surround you with love, and you will be working towards oneness.

When we begin with love and become love, then we become one with the Earth.

Know that the human beings who surround you are your equals. There is no-one more than you, and there is no-one less than you. Know that animals and plants are your friends, and none are more than you or less than you. We are all the same. The illusion is seeing that we are all different. How can we be different when we are all living creatures?

To survive here, we must care for one another. Not out of pity or admiration, out of love. If oneness is the destination, then love is the emotion that takes us there.

As you move through life, you will experience many people and many things. Some you will like more than others. Know the only differences you see are the contrasts you create in your mind. When you can put all you are and all you know aside and accept what is, you will experience the freedom of being one with the Earth and all that lies beyond her. When you achieve oneness, you will feel it in your heart.

4

TRUST

If you seek enlightenment, you must trust we know the way.

When you are connecting back to the source, you will be connecting back to us. It is with us you will find the way and the strength to complete your journey back to enlightenment. If you do not trust us, then you cannot become enlightened. If you seek guidance from us, but you do not follow our instructions, you will not become enlightened. While human beings are intelligent, you are not smarter than those who created the universe and all of her elements. Therefore, if you seek enlightenment, you must trust we know the way. If on your journey you meet a guide, acknowledge that they come on behalf of us and they can show you the way.

The memories and experiences you have access to in this lifetime are like a pin drop into an infinite ocean of knowledge. If you are the diver, we are the ocean. Dive into us, and you will find what you are seeking. It will require going to great depths, depths further than you ever imagined possible, but if you trust us, we will show you the way.

It is natural for you to fear what you don't know and what you are still coming to understand. We understand this, but we ask that if we shine a light on a person, idea, or place that you use your free will to consider it. If we give something our blessing, then this is the surest sign we can provide that a venture or adventure will be a success. Success flourishes in all that we bless.

The journey to enlightenment will come with many leaps of faith. Will you leap, or will you contemplate leaping the rest of your life?

If you commit to journeying back to enlightenment, we commit to helping you. When we commit to helping you, we commit to shining a light on you, and on all that is your best possible course of destiny. We will support you in times of sunshine and rain. We will love you when you do not feel love any longer. We will hold you when the life you used to lead holds you no longer. We will teach you when the world ceases to teach you anything you do not already know.

To receive this support, however, you must trust — more than you have ever trusted anyone or anything. Your confidence in us must overcome your rational mind as your rational mind will not serve you when it comes to a leap of faith.

Sometimes the wildest and most nonsensical things you will do in your life make the most sense later on. Trust us as we trust you to make the right choices. Trust us as we trust you to make your divine impact on the Earth. Trust us as we trust you to act on our behalf. If you cannot trust us, who can you trust?

Consider it, make it so, and begin your new life with us as your guides. Life was born to be special, and you were born to be special too. If you trust us, we will show you the way.

If we ask you to leap, ensure it is wide, strong, and without a second of doubt. If you can do this, you will make the impact your heart and soul have always dreamed of.

5

SACREDNESS

Collect the items you feel you will need on your journey to enlightenment and take them with you wherever you go in the world. They will provide you with protection and guidance.

There are many sacred places on this Earth, to some of which you will travel.

When you visit these places, you will feel a sense of calm and connectedness to the Earth. You will also experience a sense of 'being there before' because you have been there before.

When you visit these places, seek out those who are spiritual masters and ask them to show you the way of their masters. What they will teach you is knowledge passed down to them over thousands of years.

They will have recipes, unique mixtures, antidotes, and other items you will need in the new world. You will also learn practices that will assist you in becoming more connected to us. The more connected to us you become, the more connected to Earth you become and your mission here.

The holy lands I ask you to consider visiting are India, Tibet, South America, Africa, and Russia. There are many more, of course, but only in the harshest environments do the strongest elements grow.

What people from these countries do that Western countries do not is worship the ground they walk on. They respect nature and the Earth. They have learned how to live off the land, but understand that to live off the land; they must also put back what they have taken.

When I speak of these countries, I do not speak of their cities or their leaders; I speak of their healers. These are the people you must find, and often it will mean traveling to the most remote areas to seek them out.

As you grow and learn, you will come to appreciate that sacred items hold magic. You will understand this more as you learn about other cultures and the sacred objects they hold dear. Collect the items you feel you will need on your journey to enlightenment and take them with you wherever you go in the world. They will provide you with protection and guidance.

All you can see and what remains unseen are two very different things. It is the hidden world you are now seeing, and it is your trust in what is unseen that will show you the way.

Life does not always need to be explained to have value. It is what cannot be explained that is pure magic. Treat magic with the same respect you treat science, and you will see her glory and all she may reveal to you.

6

SHEDDING

If you can become the seeker, you will find all that you are looking for. But to be light enough to travel that far and to such depths, you must shed.

To become enlightened, you must shed. You must shed your worldly possessions until all you have left is all you care about, a few key things. You must release the relationships you do not need, which do not serve you.

You must shed all that you are now and all that you are not. To find your true self, you must know and understand all that you are not. To find your true self, you must shed the identity you have today and who you planned on being tomorrow. You must discard any future dreams and goals connected to a life of accumulation. You must shed anything and everything from the human world that ties you to any particular outcome.

To find enlightenment, you must seek enlightenment and be prepared to sacrifice and leave all that you are now behind.

Think of it as setting off on a pilgrimage to a higher plane, to a location you've never been to before or to a place so remote that only a few have ever been there. You are a traveler, and you are seeking the mountaintop, the center of the jungle, the place where it all began.

If you can become the seeker, you will find all that you are seeking, but to be light enough to travel that far and to such depths, you must shed. There is no point taking all you have now into tomorrow as you do not need it. What you must learn is all that you seek lies not in the world around you, but inside of you.

Enlightenment is about finding the light within, not searching for the light in a person, situation, or experience. From today, begin a process of shedding. Shed all of the things you do not need so you can see and understand all that is valuable to you. Cull all of what you have down to a precious few objects you hold dear or genuinely need. Move through your home shedding until all you have left is what you value; remembering that your identity does not lie in things; it lies in you.

Next, begin looking at the people in your life. Think about those you love and those you do not. Keep those you love and who are supportive of you and shed those who are not. We understand this sounds overly simplified, but it is not. There are simply those who love you and those who do not. Keep only those people who support your journey to enlightenment and shed those who believe the earthly plane is a better place for you. On any journey, you need supporters who can encourage you to keep moving when the path gets rocky. These are the people who you value and who value you. Keep these precious few.

Next, shed the work that is not good for you. Once again, we understand this may sound simplified, but it is not. There merely is work that is good for you and your soul and work that is not. If your work is not right for you, shed it and find something new that elevates you. Not all jobs are glorious, but some will be more suited to you than others. Seek out those jobs and throw your heart and soul into them.

Remember that the path to enlightenment will not be easy. To travel light, first, you must shed. Shedding means losing the identity you have wrapped up in things. Things are not who you are; you are who you are. If you can shed all that no longer brings you value, you will feel lighter, freer and will feel more comfortable setting off on your spiritual journey.

Free yourself up so you can leave tomorrow, today, in a week or in a month. Do what you need to, and once you start the process, everything will immediately become easier as shedding is self-perpetuating.

As you release objects, people, and work from your life, thank them for their contribution, then let them go. Letting go is like releasing an anchor so the ship may become free again. Therefore, see shedding not as a negative, but as a positive and possible opportunity that could change your life.

Begin today as tomorrow will always remain as tomorrow if you let it be this way. Life will not wait for you as life continues no matter what. Be kind to yourself and those you are releasing, but then let go and never look back. On the journey ahead, when you are light, and the possessions and people you carry are few, you will feel free, boundless, and weightless, which is how all journeys should be. The lighter you are, the more you will enjoy the journey.

7

MEDITATION

There is no ideal practice, time or place to meditate. There are however ideal practices, times and places for you.

When we meditate, we free our mind and expand it in a bid to understand more about life and our place in the universe. When we meditate, we take our 'Open' sign and change it to 'Closed' for as long as we can manage. Meditation time is time to clear our mind and begin preparing for our next minute, hour, day, or eternity.

As soon as we close our eyes, we signal we are ready to take a journey to another plane. How far or how widely we travel is dependant on how willing we are to let our heart and soul take over. The mind may drive the bus on our Earth days, but it is the heart and soul that allows us to take flight.

What you must decide is how you wish to fly. Do you wish to fly like an owl or eagle, as a human being or a butterfly? Or do you want to be the wind, flying across the mountain tops?

Flight is possible for all creatures, and it is possible for you to fly as any being you wish to be when you are in the spirit world. How you fly, who you fly as and when you fly are all up to you. Any experience can be created in a meditative state.

To experience flight, at the beginning of your meditation or journey, ask to experience life as the flying creature or any creature that interests you. Flight does not always mean leaving the ground, however. Flight can also mean feeling and being free.

There are, of course, many ways and paths to enlightenment. Meditation is one practice that will help make your journey more fluid. If I were to recommend the ideal meditative practice for enlightenment, I could not. It depends on the individual, their past, future, and present selves. I can only urge you to meditate daily and to the level of time and depth that your mind and body are physically able.

What you must understand is you do not need to meditate on top of a mountain to find enlightenment. You do not need to fast or sit in a cave, waiting for the light to come. Enlightenment is the culmination of many practices and a sustained focus on stripping back all that you are to become nothing and then who you will be.

There is no ideal method, time, or place to meditate. There are, however, excellent practices, times, and locations for you. If five minutes per day, morning and night, allow you to quiet your mind, then this shall be your practice until you can manage ten minutes morning and night. I am not suggesting you build up over time to a day in a cave; what I am suggesting is your mind must be trained to focus.

Think of your pre-meditative mind as a kitten ready to play. There is no focus there. The only focus a kitten has is on playing, eating, sleeping, and what is moving directly in front of it. When we meditate, we do not focus on what is right in front of us, we seek to broaden our view until we can see everything, but not be involved in everything. When we meditate, we are the conscious observer, neither here nor there, disconnected not connected.

The more we meditate, the more our kitten can mature into a young cat that is better able to observe their entire environment. As the cat grows, so does the focus. The more we can concentrate on meditation, the more we can clear away our distractions, put away our toys, and focus on what our life here really is and what it means.

The mind is like a muscle that must be trained, except in this instance, we're not training it to be more active, we're training it to be less active. The less active our mind becomes, the more we can see. The more we can 'see,' the more we can find our way to a new place.

If you never meditated in your life, your mind would be like a sieve overflowing with flour. Because the sieve is too full, it cannot do its job of sifting the flour; therefore, no cakes will be made. If we meditate daily and gently shake our flour through our sieve, we allow ourselves to process and release any thoughts, feelings, and actions we have from our night or day. To meditate is to release. To practice meditation daily ensures your sieve will never become too full to use or too heavy for you to hold.

If I may continue using the cooking analogy, think of enlightenment as the most beautiful cake you have ever seen. To look at, it is stunningly simple, to taste it is to eat something unforgettable and to touch it, it is light and fluffy to hold. To bake a cake like this, the baker has dedicated many years of practice. Mastery does not come in minutes; mastery is made.

For the baker to know what the ingredients of the cake are, he must explore far and wide to find ingredients that are to his taste and the quality he wishes to deliver. He understands the quality of the ingredients defines the end taste, the look, and the feeling of the cake. The baker knows there is no point making a cake and icing it to look beautiful if what's inside does not taste good or satisfy the recipient.

If you seek enlightenment, you must not take any shortcuts. You must find the practices, ideas, knowledge, and routines that allow you to free your mind, and meditation is one of these practices. Meditation helps make the master.

With your ingredients, know there will be trial and error. The path to enlightenment cannot be bought or shown. It is your cake and your journey. While you may learn from others who have come before you, their recipe is not your recipe, nor should it be. Enlightenment, while an attractive destination, is still only a destination. The beauty of enlightenment is the process your mind, heart, and soul took to get there. What you create in your life, what goes into the oven, and what comes out must make you proud. It must have pushed you beyond your comfort zone as genuine pride is born out of conquering fear.

Meditation is a foundation practice that helps a human being build to enlightenment, but it is not the only practice. It is one ingredient of the beautiful cake you aspire to make. Seek out the ingredients you believe you will need and try them out in your life. Bend your mind and your routine to incorporate them.

There are many millions of cakes in the world, and yours can be what you wish it to be. Enlightenment is simply the word we use to describe the feeling of baking something so life-changing you will remember it for eternity.

To become enlightened is to realize all that you are, all that you were and all that you are not. When you know what you are and what you are not, there is a space left in the middle for what you could become. Enlightenment is baking the cake of your dreams, and knowing every ingredient was added with love, wisdom, and care. The cake you leave behind is your legacy. The art form of what you have created is the culmination of your life on Earth.

True enlightenment is baking the cake, but not needing to eat it, because baking it was enough.

8

MAGNITUDE

When we become one again we will be free. When we act with knowledge, with love and with wisdom we can turn our solo journey into a journey for many.

When you act or commit yourself to something, you may not realize the magnitude of your actions until much later. When you work daily, with intent, what you create is a ripple effect that can sweep the world.

If you wish to become enlightened, you can be a rock sitting next to a pond, silent and alone, or you can be the rock that drops into the pond and creates ripples. If you want to make an impact on Earth while you are here, be the rock that creates ripples. Use your journey to take other people along with you.

Enlightenment is not only for a few to receive, it is for everybody, but not everybody is aware they can strive for enlightenment. Most assume it is for a select few and those who meditate in monasteries. It is not, it is for all, and it is our wish for all on Earth to achieve this state.

Therefore, if you have set off on the path to enlightenment, share what you are doing with others. Explain that every practice is different, and no one practice is right. Define the destination and what it may feel like to get there. Translate it into the language you speak, and for the people you are speaking to.

A long time ago, the Earth and all of her people were enlightened. However, over time, as we have believed we have grown smarter, we have become more arrogant. The more arrogant and self-consumed we become, the less enlightened we are.

Enlightenment is finding our way back to the beginning, to our original intent and meaning. It is not being wrapped up and consumed by the world, but stepping back and becoming aligned again with the universe and its creators.

Do not feel this is a journey just for adults alone. Children are the closest to enlightened we have on the planet. Share your journey with the children in your life and encourage them to find their way back to a more enlightened state.

When we become one again, we will be free. When we act with knowledge, love, and with wisdom, we can turn our solo journey into a path for many. When we document our journey, we can share it with many others. When we become free, we can free many others.

Life on Earth can mean slavery or freedom for many. The rules you set yourselves do not exist. The people in power in your world encourage hopelessness. All you must do is realize that no-one is holding you back except yourself.

What you see in the media and on TV is an elaborate sideshow to distract you from what is truly going on, which is the consumption of Earth. If you are always watching the action, you miss the inaction. If you always listen to what you are told to hear, you are missing everything you are not hearing. What is seen in your world is what they want you to see.

Look for what is unseen, unheard, and not felt, and you will find your answers. Amongst all the noise and commotion, look for the silence and space, and that is where you can find peace.

Help those you know realize that there is another way to live than living by the rules of others who only live for consumption and accumulation. There are respectful ways to live that feel good and fill us up, but we must look for them.

The actions we take now daily create a ripple effect of tremendous magnitude, but only if we drop the rock in the first place. If the rock sits by the pond, there are no ripples. It is just a rock. If the rock drops in the pond, many will feel it.

Which rock will you be?

9

SANITY

Do not sacrifice who you are to play a role because eventually all the masks you wear will be forced to fall.

When we are sane, we are clear on who we are and what we want. When we are insane, the world is a mix of what is clear and unclear, but we cannot tell the difference. If you wish to be clear and sane about your actions, beliefs, and ideas, then the path to enlightenment can take you there.

What we find in our lives on Earth is that we play many roles so we can be many things to many people. This idea is the very definition of insanity as one person cannot be so many things for so long and not experience a breakdown of sorts. The more we can realize all of the roles we play, the more we can separate them and put down each mask we wear one at a time.

We live in a world where we are expected to be great at everything we do. We are supposed to be the perfect mother, father, friend, colleague, brother, sister, daughter, and son. We know we cannot be great at all of them all at once, yet we try and fail. We try to be brilliant at everything, and we lose who we truly are along the way. We cannot hold so many personalities and responsibilities within us and not expect for the masks we wear to fall or fragment. There will come a time where you will realize you can no longer carry ten masks and keep swapping between as this is insanity.

What you must do instead is begin placing each mask down, one at a time until there is just one. It does not mean losing your role as a mother, daughter, son, colleague, etc. It means realizing you cannot achieve perfection in all of them without sacrificing all of yourself. Dropping your masks does not mean failure; it is accepting that perfection is not achievable and not something we should strive for because it does not exist. What we must strive for is to be our true selves, not actors playing many roles in one day. Realize you are not a mother, father, son, or daughter. You are a human being who happens to have or be a mother, father, son, or daughter.

Do not sacrifice who you are to play a role because eventually, all the masks you wear will be forced to fall. You do not have to be great at everything. What you must strive for is to be your one true self.

We can start putting the masks down when we realize we are holding many masks. Once we understand we are holding many masks, we can begin to remind ourselves that perfection across all is not achievable. We can then allow ourselves to breathe easier, knowing that we are not perfect, nor should we be. We are but one person who happens to be many things. The problem on Earth is that we strive to be too many different people within the one body. This way of life is not sustainable, and eventually, we will fall due to exhaustion.

Put your masks down and accept that the only person you should strive to be is who you are, all roles aside. This will be your journey to enlightenment, stripping back all you are, and the many versions of yourself you contain until there is just one mask. Enlightenment is being able to put that last mask down and realize we are not a human being playing a part, we are a spirit that is endless, boundless, and our potential should not be limited to such one-dimensional things. Reduce your masks until you have just one, then we will focus on how you put the last mask down. This is the final test.

You are most sane when you are speaking with just one voice and one identity. You are the least sane when you are playing many roles for many people. Human beings joke that the path to enlightenment is a journey for those who have gone insane. We would say that the path to enlightenment is the journey for those who are looking for sanity, and if they persist, they will find it.

10

LIGHT

Remember that the lighter you become, the more darkness you will attract.

On the path to enlightenment, your objective is to bring more light into your being and also to connect back to the light.

You will be driving the darkness out of you, so it doesn't have anywhere left to live. Doing this is not an easy task as life on Earth is both light and dark, and life can naturally become darker sometimes. What you must learn to do is tame the darkness, so the energy you use to move forward is born from light, not dark. Where light energy aims to protect, uplift, and heal, dark energy will attempt to drag you down and wound you so that you may never get up again. Dark energy feeds on those who cannot protect themselves and lives by you dying, inside and out. To protect yourself from dark energy, you must coat yourself in light and keep bringing more light in.

How you bring more light in is simple: only engage in those activities and with those people who contribute light. What you must understand is that light also attracts darkness as light is the most attractive meal for those who live in the dark.

To protect yourself from darkness, you must ask that the universe only brings you those who are bathed in light. To end darkness, you must be so bursting with light that it is too confronting for those who live in the dark. They will choose not to be around your energy. Just as darkness feeds on light, light drives away the dark if it is strong enough.

Think of the sunrise as it comes up. There is no denying it is the sun, and it is only a matter of time before the sunlight touches everything that exists in that hemisphere. It is the same way with light and how it affects people. At night as the sun goes down, it is only a matter of time before the darkness coats everything it sees. In the dark, you can still burn brightly even when nothing around you is. You need to be the lantern that lights the way for yourself and others. Just because the night exists does not mean you can't burn brightly in both the night and the day. Remember this.

If you need to burn brighter, engage only in activities with people who allow you to burn brighter, not try and drag you down. By spending time with those who pull you down, you are making your battles harder. By choosing to devote more time to the light, you will naturally make your days brighter and your path to enlightenment easier.

The only way to reach enlightenment is by walking towards the brightest light you can find and keep walking until you reach it. Darkness will try and persuade you to stop, telling you it is all too hard, but it is not. Darkness chooses the dark because that is where it lives. Light chooses light because it is the only place it can live. Choose high vibrational activities, practices, and people. Spending time in the light is like holding a helium balloon; there is no choice but to go up.

Remember that the lighter you become, the more darkness you will attract, but know that if you stay focused on the light you are walking towards, you cannot see the dark. Light attracts light too. Find more lightworkers on the way, and you will have a journey you love. Find darkness and spend time in the darkness, and your journey will be slow.

The path to enlightenment is simple. Locate the light, be light, and move towards the light. Know that darkness will never bring you happiness and only wastes your time. Invest your time in experiences and people who are light and who will enable you to make yourself brighter.

When in a situation you are unsure of, ask yourself, 'Will this person or experience bring more light into my life?'. If yes, you may proceed. If the answer is no, weigh up the costs to your energy short term versus long term and decide. We understand that life is not simple, but you can ask these simple questions of yourself.

11

TALKING

We believe in those who believe in us, those who wish for a better future on Earth and those who are full of courage, not air.

In today's world, we do too much talking and not enough doing. We have been taught about the power of ideas, but not enough about the power of action. When we act, we change places, things, people, and institutions. When we speak, we may inspire, but we do not always create the change we seek.

For those on the path to enlightenment, you have signed up to make change through action, and this road is not for the faint of heart. Creating action requires you to challenge who you are and who you were. It is not only speaking of what you've learned but showing how you're putting it into practice in your daily life. It is defining your dream for the Earth and then putting a plan into action for how you will contribute and help get us there.

As human beings, we are inspired by great orators, but the truly great orators also lead movements. We do not wish this to daunt you as you are already part of a movement working to change the Earth, her current circumstances, and her future. At the very least, all you must do is keep walking, talking, and taking action, and you will be helping the Earth. For those, however, who wish to make their impact here more significant, now is the time for you to put your thoughts into action. What do you want your legacy to be? How do you want to be remembered?

If who you are becoming is very different from who you were, begin making these changes in a way that is slow and steady. Slow and steady is better than a fast talker who makes no changes or impact.

In former times, human beings were great and charismatic leaders. Leaders who inspired, but also fought on the front lines with their troops. Today we reward those who are charismatic, but we do not ask them to test their beliefs by requiring them to fight on the ground with those they are trying to inspire, which is the real test of a great leader.

If a leader tells you an idea, but they are not prepared to do it themselves, they are just talking. If a leader believes in an idea enough to fully immerse themselves in it, then they are committed to both ideas and action. It is these types of leaders the Earth needs more of.

You may not want to change the entire world, but you can change the way you live or the community you live in by sharing your ideas and taking action.

If you want to change the world, we will support you in this, but only if you are willing to put yourself and your identity on the line. We believe in those who believe in us, those who wish for a better future on Earth and those who are full of courage, not air.

12

MAGIC

There is magic within all of us, we just choose not to see it.

There is magic within all of us; we just choose not to see it. We choose not to see it because as human beings, we don't tend to believe in what we can't see.

To know you are magic, you must feel you are magic. To feel you are magic, you must experience your magic. To experience magic, you must create it in your life. To do this, you must believe in the power of synchronicity. You must feel your aura and the auras of those around you. You must feel the gravity that pulls you down to the Earth and the weightlessness of what you could become. You are an incredible creature of light, and your magic will come as soon as you acknowledge this.

The path to enlightenment is not about feeling 'enlightened.' It is about realizing that despite your human form, you are not a human being; you are a spirit of endless potential, magic, and power. When you embrace this, your life will change. When you embrace the magic of spirit, you will feel the spirit within you.

Your human body is just flesh, a vehicle for you to travel around in and experience Earth. It is not who you are, and it is not who you will become. It is merely an earthly vehicle. Yes, you have eyes, ears, a nose, and a mouth, but they do not define you. Yes, you may have a title, a piece of land, a family, partner, and friends, but none of these makes you who you are. They are all parts of your experience here on Earth and elements interacting with one another. When you realize you are not your body or your experience, you will know how limitless and free you are.

For some, Earth feels like a trap. For others, Earth is a place to be powerful. Neither are correct as those views mean you are only seeing the world as most do now, the only life we lead and have led.

Earth is a playground of massive proportions. A place to learn, an adventure to be experienced, but remember it is not who you are. The real magic you wish to experience lies within you, and in the many lives you have led before. What we want you to do is take all of that knowledge and the power of your spirit and bring it to Earth.

You are all healers sent down to Earth to heal this place and the people you meet on the path. Use your time and experience to heal and bring light. You are all light beings, but sometimes you become distracted by your body. You only see what's in front of you, not what's around you, behind you, underneath, and within you. You are all magic, but you must choose to accept this magic into your life. Let the spirit back in, and you will see a tremendous change. Remember that your body is just a body and a vehicle for you to have this experience.

Knowing this information may be a lot to take on, but let these ideas sift through you like sand falling from your hand. Let it envelop you, let it change your experience, and you will find yourself living in a new Earth.

13

HOPE

We need hope to live, but sometimes hope makes living harder.

Hope is what keeps us going, but our hopes can also be dashed. When we have hope, we believe there is a brighter future for ourselves and for those we love. Hope is an emotion, but it is also a dream, a picture painted by us of something we wish for. The challenge with hope is sometimes what we want isn't good for us, nor is it destined to happen. We need hope to live, but sometimes hope makes living harder.

When our hopes are dashed, or a situation does not go as planned, we can feel deflated and lost. What we had been hoping or wishing for no longer exists. It is for this reason that while we must invest ourselves in hope, we should not invest all we have in hope.

Hope will not keep us warm at night, nor should it. Hope will not protect us from a storm or the negative experiences in our lives. If we wish to be enlightened, we must recognize that hope is for those who are attached to an outcome. The purpose of enlightenment is to know that the outcome is ourselves. We are a diamond in the process of being polished and one that cannot be bought, sold, or transformed into another precious jewel. We are who we are, and realizing all the beauty we have within us and can create is the journey we are completing.

We are not made better by another human being, nor can another human being complete us. We are already complete when we begin because we are a soul. If we can recognize our infinite potential, we can work on realizing this while we are on Earth. What we must remember is that while hope is needed here on Earth, hope is still an earthly idea. In the sky, we are just what we are, and we never wish for anything more or anything less.

If you wish to become enlightened, you must realize enlightenment isn't a journey to become more beautiful. Enlightenment is the understanding you are already beautiful and are working towards a goal the entire Earth will benefit from.

The real lesson is realizing that while you may be a raw diamond here on Earth, you are not for sale, and you never will be. It is not the beauty of the diamond that makes it unique; it is the process it has gone through to manifest itself. It is the diamond's raw potential and its constant evolution that makes it unique and valuable. When you leave this life, you will understand what lies beyond Earth, and you will see that we are all diamonds waiting to be revealed.

We are all diamonds. The trees are diamonds, as are animals and people. Even under the harshest conditions, we cannot be destroyed because we are all spirits that have been here many times before. We have the strength of a diamond and the beauty of a precious gem, both of which have taken thousands of years to evolve.

When you see other people, animals, and trees, see diamonds. See something worth uncovering and protecting. See the raw potential in all things and appreciate the journey it has taken for each being to get to where they are today. And when you have hope, hope for a future where all of the Earth's diamonds are treated equally. A future where we do not cut each other down, where we cannot be bought or sold or where some diamonds are worth more than others. Hope is what we wish for. It is positive, but it can also work against us if we hope for things and not for people. Hope for evolution, whatever that may bring, and you will never be disappointed.

14

SPEED

What we must learn and remember is that enlightenment isn't a product. It is a process and ultimately a destination that can take some human beings many lifetimes to reach.

The path to enlightenment is not a thirty-day course, nor should it be.

We live in a world where we want everything delivered quickly and on a silver platter, with no investment of ourselves other than money to acquire it. You cannot buy enlightenment, nor can you speed it up. You can, however, purify your life and existence as much as possible, distilling all that you are until the path ahead is much clearer.

Human beings are sold the dream of speed, and we are continually trying to speed everything up. We use our knowledge to 'hack the system' and then we sell that knowledge on to those who want the greatest results in the shortest amount of time. While you may become more enlightened than what you were, enlightenment cannot be found in this way. As a society, we must learn to have more patience, patience with ourselves, each other, and the time it takes to get somewhere or do something. We cannot expect everything to be bundled into a package we can buy.

In earlier times, people believed you needed to meditate on a mountaintop to seek enlightenment or undertake a pilgrimage that needed all the energy of your mind and body. Neither of these options ever guaranteed a result, but people were happy to try them to get closer to what they were seeking to find.

If you wish to find enlightenment, do not assume it will be a speedy process. All that you are cannot be stripped back in a defined period. All that you can be cannot be discovered in a specified period.

All that you may discover in thirty-days is a willingness to seek enlightenment and to begin doing some of the many practices that may help get you there.

If you wish to seek enlightenment, first strive to understand what this means to you, to others, to those throughout history, and ultimately what it will mean for you if you find it. Enlightenment is not for all, but we wish it were. If enlightenment is what you still want for after you study it, then seek to find it, but also know that it will test you. You must be prepared to lose all that you are to become all that you could be. While this sounds easy, we must remember the role ego plays in our life. Ego is not an easy friend to lose, and it will continue to present tests to entice and engage you.

What we must understand is that enlightenment isn't a product. It is a process and ultimately a destination that can take human beings many lifetimes to reach. If you are serious about enlightenment, you will accept that it may take more than your lifetime to achieve and may be something the next version of you also takes on.

We do not tell you this to scare you. We are only revealing the true nature of a process and journey as old as time itself. Respect the process, and do not take shortcuts. The destination is worth the journey, and the journey is worth the destination.

15

BELIEF

Ideas and people need those who believe in them. Otherwise, the words of the few are not heard by the ears of the many.

Belief is what we have when we will something into existence. Belief is what makes ideas possible. Without belief, people are forced to do things on their own, trying to make a small difference. For belief to create power, many people need to believe, not just a few.

Many people will not believe in this book, and few will see its transformative power. Over the centuries, we have seen many great artists create paintings or pieces of art that did not become famous until the few believers became many over time. It is the same way with some of the most significant books and pieces of poetry ever written. For many creators, belief accumulates over time, and for some, that time is centuries. Rest assured, those creators in the places they live now know the transformative power of their pieces, and they are proud of what they've achieved.

It is the same experience with modern works. Many people are trying to transform the planet, yet the many who could believe in them do not. They sit on the sidelines, waiting for others to believe before they do. At this time, we need human beings to take a leap of faith and trust that what we say is coming. The Earth's resources are being used, ground up, and burned. It is only a matter of time before those resources are gone, and we have nothing left to use, ground-up, or burn. Then what becomes of human beings? Human beings with no power, nothing to keep you warm, and no energy to produce the things you say you need?

When this time comes, we will see humanity tested. This is what we push you to realize as those on the enlightened path already do that you not need all that you have to become enlightened. You do not need all the things you carry around with you, emotionally and physically. All you need and all you will eventually have is your true self.

Until that time, believe in and share the ideas you know will contribute to helping save the Earth. Know that the effort you put in now will make a difference. In a world of non-believers, be someone who openly believes in transformative ideas as they arise and not someone who lets these ideas age for centuries before they are taken seriously.

Most of all, believe in yourself. When everything can be taken away in a second, through environmental transformation, natural disasters, war, or famine, believe that all you need in this world is you. Help others find their true selves so that they may also weather the storm when it arrives.

Know that if you undertake this path of stripping back that you have our support, day or night, stormy or sunny, raining or windy. While there are a lot of things on Earth that are an illusion, the destruction of the Earth is not. You are living on a resource that is slowly being eaten up.

Ideas and people need those who believe in them. Otherwise, the words of the few are not heard by the ears of the many. Know this and support those ideas and people who need your support and belief. Without them, the Earth will die a swift death with thousands of potential solutions lying in ideas, books, art, and people who remain transformative, but unused.

16

PATIENCE

The hardest journeys we will undertake are the ones we do on our own, yet they are the most rewarding.

When we begin a new journey in our lives, we must be mindful to pack patience. Patience is what lies in between the journey's beginning and its completion.

It is easy to say you will do something and even easier to dream about it, but it is harder to complete the vision when you need to sacrifice things to get it. Patience is one of the most challenging lessons we learn during our time on Earth. It is never easy, nor is it hard.

During times of trauma or hardship, we must be patient that the light is coming. When we are learning a new skill, trade, or practice, we must be patient because learning something new takes time and patience. We must be patient with ourselves and with others. When we are under stress, it is wise for us to be patient with everyone and everything around us. If we can do this, our load will be lighter. If we cannot do this in times of stress, we can damage the bridges we have already built.

Human beings are very talented at dreaming up exciting ideas and things to achieve. We are, however not as skilled at putting in the work. The work is the part that's not glamorous, which can be getting up early in the morning to write a book, staying late to practice the guitar after the other musicians have gone home, or going into the forest with just a pencil and a notebook to draw what you find.

The hardest journeys we will undertake are the ones we do on our own, yet they are the most rewarding. If we give ourselves time and patience, we can learn anything we wish to. Patience is waiting for the rain to come or the sun to come out. Patience is throwing something out there into the universe that you've worked hard on and waiting to see what comes back.

Without patience, there is no sweetness in the anticipation. We live in a society where we want everything now. Why have everything now though, when you can wait until you are genuinely ready for it? Patience is a blessing and virtue. It is also necessary for us to appreciate what we have and what we've worked so hard for.

Work hard and then be patient. Keep working hard and keep being patient. Patience comes to those who are happy to wait. When we aren't rewarded for our patience, what we are waiting for was potentially not meant to be.

Live the life you want, create the life you want, and put in the hard work to get there. Patience is what sits in the middle. Enjoy it, ponder it, and use it as an opportunity to make your mind even stronger.

17

CONCENTRATION

If you wish to undertake the path to enlightenment, you will need vast amounts of concentration as the path does not bring excitement and revelations every day.

When you first begin something, you are very focused. As time goes on, your attention and focus wane. This is a natural occurrence, but one to be aware of as even the greatest of intentions can end in inaction when our lives become busy.

If you wish to undertake the path to enlightenment, you will need vast amounts of concentration as the path does not bring excitement and revelations every day. There are many days when you will feel dejected, alone, without support or understanding, but this is the nature of the path to enlightenment.

You need to concentrate and focus because what you are trying to do is step away from all you hold dear, which may mean learning many different spiritual practices, or perhaps just one such as meditation. In anything you do, you must be comfortable sitting in the silence, longer than what makes you feel comfortable. Longer than the time you are usually comfortable sitting in the darkness. You will be required to undertake tasks that will need you to get up early, stay up late, choose your priorities, and then re-align them.

We are not saying you are choosing a life of solitude, but there is an element of solitude you will need to find space for in your life. The path to enlightenment is not a part-time project; it is a way of living, being, and breathing. The more you can open yourself up to us, the more you will intuitively know what you must do to reach us and the destination you are seeking.

Do not expect to reach enlightenment in a month, a year, or a decade. It may take your whole life or even a few lifetimes depending on how quickly you can learn. This journey is not for the faint of heart or for those who lack concentration or dedication, but you can learn both if you decide to undertake this journey.

Without focus, we cannot learn. Without dedication, we cannot commit to the length of time needed to change. See your spiritual practice not as something that is out of the ordinary. See it as part of your life and as something as necessary as breathing, eating, drinking, and sleeping. Then it does not require concentration; it is merely a part of you, your system, and your life.

When you lose concentration, you've lost focus on the task at hand. The speed at which you undertake and complete this journey is up to you. With concentration, the learning you undertake can reach your soul at a deeper level. Without concentration, learning is like watching TV, entertaining but not life-changing.

Make your spiritual practices and routines a part of your life, and you will enjoy every moment of the journey because it will no longer feel like a journey, it will be your life.

18

DESTINY

When the universe makes plans for us, it takes into account our potential and what we could achieve. This is very different from what our human selves think we can achieve. Universal potential is infinite, human potential is a great job.

Your destiny is your destination. It is the place planned for you to end up. It is your role here on Earth and the role you were destined to play. The question is, will you embrace your destiny once you know what it is?

What occurs on Earth is that the plan the universe has for us differs from the role we plan for ourselves. It is not a bad thing, but what we miss out on is by planning an earthly role for ourselves is the greater part we can play. When the universe makes plans for us, it takes into account our potential and what we could achieve, which is very different to what our human selves think we can achieve. Our universal potential is infinite; human potential is a great job. As you can see, there is a big difference.

If you trust us to uncover your universal potential, we will guide you there. If you do not trust us, we can only help you as much as you will allow us to. If you believe you are destined for a job, then that is what you will do in this life. If you know you are destined to be more than this, and you are willing to be guided, we will guide you to your destiny. We cannot do this though unless you allow us to.

We are always given a destiny we are ready for, but if our mind and the universe do not align, then this potential future is forced to wait until the next life. Where the opportunity lies is if you allow your destiny to happen and be guided by us, you will achieve more than you ever thought possible or dreamed of.

What we require of you, though, is to be open-minded enough to know and understand that anything is possible when you work with us. We need you also to recognize that a 'job' or career may not be your destiny. We, of course, know you will need to earn money during your time here, but do not ever think that your fate is to work behind a desk. Where we fail ourselves is by assuming that we cannot be more than what we are now, which is a shame as there is always time to be more, do more and see more. There is always time to accept your destiny rather than take a job.

If you do not know what your destiny is, we can guide you there. That is our job, but you must be open-minded enough to know that what we present you with will be a raw diamond, unpolished and unlikely to fit in a box. What you do with this raw diamond is up to you, and whether you choose the raw diamond or a job is an indication of whether you need more time to grow here on Earth before you embrace your destiny.

For those who embrace rather than reject their destiny, the path will be bumpy but exhilarating. For those who choose a job, your life will be what you expect it to be. To do something great, you must leave comfort behind and exchange it for discomfort. To do something you will be remembered for, you must leave money and trade it for the unknown rewards fulfilling your destiny will bring.

19

MASTERY

Choose to become a master at only that which you love, as being a master of what you loathe only brings pain and a slowing of time.

To be a master of something, you must put in many hours of work and practice. To be a master, you must consider yourself to be a master, but this is a leap of faith for some. During our lives, we are all masters of something. Some things we choose and some we don't. Some of us become good at things we don't enjoy, some of us become good at things we do enjoy.

If you are a master at something you don't enjoy, now is the time to move away from it. Why subject yourself to more pain by staying in something you do not love? When the master becomes the slave, then it is no longer mastery; it is a slavery of the highest form.

If you do love something and you could become a master of it, pursue it. If you have found something you love that could you be a master at, what is holding you back from taking it over? These are all things you must think about. As they say, life is too short to spend time doing what you do not love. Life is also too long to be doing what you do not love as the time for those in something they do not enjoy goes on forever. If you can break away from that thing, even if it is just a tear in a piece of paper, it is better than nothing as a tear can eventually become a piece of paper that is torn in half.

We have a belief that life on Earth must be endured. It does not and should not. We have freedom beyond our wildest dreams, yet we do not see it or embrace it. Instead, we endure the work we have become a master at, and we say, 'Well, I am a master at it, I should continue.' Why? It does not bring you joy in your heart, mind, or soul. Does it bring joy to your ego? Your ego is a tough customer to satisfy. The ego will never be satisfied. It will always push you for more. The ego never takes into consideration what you love or do not love; it only takes into account whether you satisfy society and those around you. What if I told you that society would never be satisfied because society is unhappy? What if I told you that you would never satisfy the people around you because they are most likely also unhappy?

Therefore, to be a master at something you do not enjoy, you only sacrifice yourself to invisible masters who will never be satisfied. Life is too short and too long to do what you do not love. Life is too short and too long to be a master at something that has turned you into a slave. Think of the piece of paper and begin with a small tear that has the potential to turn into a sheet of paper torn in half. Do not see this as tearing up your career. Instead, see it as tearing away from something you mastered but now do not love.

It is only through creating space in our lives that we leave enough room for something new to enter. Remember this when your ego tells you to leave the paper alone. Remember this when your friends and family tell you to do the same. It is your sheet of paper, your life, and your choice as to what you master and when. The carpenter need not stay a carpenter his whole life because that is what he has been trained to do. The carpenter can become an artist, but only if he tears himself away from carpentry and moves into art.

Life evolves, we evolve, and it is naturally part of the process. Choose to become a master at only that which you love, as being a master of what you loathe only brings pain and a slowing of time. Remember this.

MONEY

A life spent focusing on money is a higher form of slavery.

The relationship you have with money can be like the relationships you have with human beings, good and bad. What you must realize is that money is just a service. Money allows us to buy what we need, but money should not be able to buy us.

If we have a good relationship with money, we will use our money to buy what we need, not what we want. I am not saying you do not deserve holidays or treats for your hard work. I am saying we make ourselves slaves to something that doesn't exist so we can buy things we don't need. We spend our entire lives working for things we don't need, and we miss out on what we could have: a life.

If you can realize your relationship with money and define if it is good, bad, or average, then you will know if you need to improve your relationship with money. If your relationship with money is good, how can you make it better? Unfortunately, more money means more work. If more work is what you want, then please keep going, but if it is not, then consider how much money you need to live the life you want.

If your relationship with money is bad, think about why it is bad. Think about who is in charge when it comes to your money. Is it you or is it your bank balance? I would also encourage you to reflect on how you would like your relationship with money to be. I am not asking, 'What things do you want?' I am asking about the flow of money in your life.

If your relationship with money is average, think about what you have to gain bettering your relationship with money. Money can't buy you happiness, but having what you need can buy your time back.

Life is too short and too long to have a bad relationship with money. Figure out how much money you need to buy what you need, and this will give you a foundation for beginning your re-assessment of the part money plays in your life.

Human beings were not supposed to spend their lives being slaves to things that do not exist. Money has most humans on their knees. If you choose to spend your life working for money and things that you do not need, then this is your choice. Or you could decide to spend your time only accumulating the money you need to live a healthy, balanced life where you see friends, family and have more time to have fun.

A life spent focusing on money is a higher form of slavery. Free yourself from the chains of this illusion, and you will see an improvement in your life. Money is not your boss or your owner, but the right relationship means you can be friends with money.

Assess what you need and work with that amount of money. What you need might mean enough to eat, drink, enough for study, to see friends and family, and sufficient funds for a holiday. What every person needs will be different; the key is establishing what a 'want' versus a 'need' is. When you realize the difference, your relationship with money will improve.

21

FEARS

The only way to break down a fear is to get to know it. It is by getting to know it that you can take its power away.

Fears are what hold us back, but they can also move us forward, depending on how we use them.

If you are fearful of something, ask why. One of the biggest mistakes humans make is never asking why a particular fear exists. The only way to break down fear is to get to know it. It is by getting to know it that you can take its power away.

If you are heading off on a new adventure, do not fear for your safety. Only if you have not planned adequately will you fail. Do not fear what is new as what is new eventually becomes old. If you follow the path laid out for you, you cannot fail.

If something scares you, there is a high chance you will be good at it. If you wake up in the morning with a mixture of excitement and fear, you know you are pushing your boundaries. If, however, you wake up knowing every part of what will happen today, then life may have become boring for you.

The challenge is that all new pursuits and adventures require a leap of faith. You can, of course, make thousands of tiny steps towards the chasm, but eventually, when you get to the edge, you need to be able to leap.

If you do leap, the rewards will be plenty, both mentally, physically, and spiritually. If you do not leap, then you will shoulder regrets that may last a lifetime. You will always wonder what could have been had you decided it was worth overcoming your fears.

Sometimes it is easier to stick with what we know, but it is not better to stick with what we know just because we know it. You will see when a leap of faith is required because there will be no-where else for you to go except across or back. We hope you will jump across, as what you have to lose is nothing compared to what you have to gain.

Fears are nothing but words, beliefs, and accumulated anxiety from a life half lived. When we fully embrace life and enjoy it for what it is, there is no fear because we come to love the unexpected. Cherish the opportunity to grow and get ready to leap. If you fall, the price will be no more than what you pay to stay in a life that does not push you or help you grow. You grow even by attempting to leap.

Do not fear others' opinions about your leap. Do not pay others' attention when they speak of your pursuits. Some choose to stay in the safety of their backyard, never venturing out to be free. Never risking what they have; to find out what they could gain. Life is an adventure, but only if you make it so. The larger the leap, the faster you'll reach your destination.

It is worth keeping in mind when we speak of a leap, that we are not saying to pick the widest part of the chasm and hope for the best. Find the smallest gap as the result will likely be the same.

22

MARVELLING

If you wish to find enlightenment, you must be prepared to see yourself as not more unique than anyone else, but as unique as everything else.

To experience life to its fullest, we must marvel at everything around us. Everything we see, hear, feel, and smell has come from something born of Earth. Sometimes when our lives get too busy, we forget to marvel at the wonders that surround us. Sometimes we feel like it is only our life that matters: our way to work, our way of life, and our way of being. It is not ideal to think this way as we are one tiny part of a web of millions and billions of creatures and things. On the path to enlightenment, you will experience more wonder than you ever thought possible. Wonder is one of the rewards of undertaking this journey.

On the path to enlightenment, you will begin to see the Earth in a new way. You will notice the Earth is alive in a way you never saw before. You will hear the trees whispering to you and the wind telling you stories. You will see that even ants have places they need to go.

It is when we understand we are not more important than another will we begin to feel we are a part of something bigger. It is only when we know we are a part of something larger than us that we can then start to tap into universal knowledge.

There are many gods worshipped on Earth, but there is only one path to enlightenment. Those caught up in living a good life on Earth forget the path to enlightenment is a journey back to the sky. It is a way one seeks only when they are ready, which tends to be in their last life on Earth. A spiritual seeker may have been building to this or had many attempts in previous lifetimes as this is the way.

If you wish to find enlightenment, you must be prepared to see yourself as not more unique than anyone else, but as unique as everything else. It is only through accepting our place in the web of life can we eventually ascend above it.

Do not measure yourself by how far you've come, although this is nice occasionally. Instead, measure yourself by how far you still have to go. Looking at your progress in this way will allow you to take your place while seeing the bigger picture and beginning the process of re-learning life all over again, which is the path of enlightenment.

23

ROADS

The path is not glorious or wondrous, but the outcome is.

On the path to enlightenment, no one road will take you there. There are many.

When people think of the path to enlightenment, they believe there are specific things they must do. There is not. There is no one road or set of processes a human being must do to become enlightened. Enlightenment isn't about adding things to your life; it's about stripping life back until all you can see is what matters: spirit.

On Earth, we carry everything with us. In addition to our stresses, worries, personalities, and egos, we also carry our possessions and our stories. If you wish to become enlightened, all of this will be too heavy for the journey. If you do not shed, you will be forced to discover this excess weight on the way.

As you set off on your journey, initially, you will not notice the extra weight you are carrying. You will only see the destination ahead, and the excitement alone will fuel you. However, once the path becomes a little harder and your feet sorer, you will realize you need to lighten your load somehow. These may be in the form of emotional releases, or you may release a possession you thought you valued, but carrying it now is not as important as reaching your destination. Whatever these releases are, you must leave them on the path and continue.

On the path to enlightenment, while the destination is important, it's the journey where you learn about yourself and what matters to you.

Over the days, nights, weeks, and months of walking, you will continue to shed. As you shed, your mind will become even clearer. What you will come to realize is there are many things you carry that you do not need, that weigh you down rather than keep you light. It is your job to figure out what to leave behind with kindness so that you may continue.

There will be some crisis of conscience, but if you do not look at the whole, and only one item at a time, the decisions you face will be far easier. Knowing that the path to enlightenment ends with only your spirit should make your decisions easier. Your spirit does not own things; it does not tell stories or have an ego. The spirit is as it always has been, the purest version of you that does not need or want for anything.

If along the way, you find it harder to let go of specific items, stories, and beliefs, then ask yourself why you find it hard to let go. Does the article, story, or belief make you who you are?

The mistake human beings make is we mix our identity up in what we own and the stories we tell about ourselves. What we own is not who we are. What we say about ourselves is not who we are and what others say about us is what they know about us; therefore, it is not who we are.

The path to enlightenment is not about gaining more, it is about stripping your life back, and we understand this is not for everybody. There will be some uncomfortable truths you will discover about yourself, which you have gained over thousands of years of past lives. There will be mistakes you've made in former lives that you will need to rectify on the way. There will be things you've done in this life that you will come face to face with on the path.

The path is not glorious or wondrous, but the outcome is. Human beings treat enlightenment like it is something to be bought. It is not. It is the single most treacherous and hardest journey on Earth. Most will turn back as soon as it gets a little hard. Few continue to the end as it is a lifetime, and sometimes more than a lifetime commitment.

In a world of instant gratification, you can see why it is not for everybody. Most will only aspire to it and talk about it, and that will be enough. For those who are serious, you can leave tomorrow, but keep in mind the weight of your pack. It is only a matter of time before you will need to start shedding. Best to do it now before you leave than to carry unnecessary weight along the way.

24

TRAVEL

When you travel, you welcome new ideas and ways of life because you expect it. Expect changes if you embark on the path to enlightenment.

The path to enlightenment requires travel, but if you cannot travel, then do it in your mind.

Seeing other places, people, plants, and animals opens our minds to other possibilities. When we travel in the real world, it is similar to the path to enlightenment because when we travel, we travel light with only a few possessions that matter to us. We need our passport, identification, money, enough clothing, but more than anything; we bring with us an attitude of change. We bring openness and a sense of oneness with those around us. Rather than walking with our head down, closed off to society from fear of having a conversation, when we travel, we walk with our head up.

When we travel, we embrace that some things may go wrong along the way, and we accept it to be so. When we are at home, we hate it when things go wrong. When we travel, we smile, and we're willing to learn about other cultures and ways of life. This is the nature of the path to enlightenment.

On the path to enlightenment, we want you to have the same lightness in your pack as you do when you travel in the real world. Take with you the same attitude of openness, oneness, and exploration. Take with you only what you need as what you truly need you will find on the path.

When you travel, you welcome new ideas and ways of life because you expect it. Expect changes if you embark on the path to enlightenment. Expect adventure, fun, and challenges. No path is ever dull or uninteresting, just as no journey overseas is dull or uninteresting.

See the path as you see travel, and you will have all you need to go and let go.

25

CHALLENGES

How you face the challenges that arise in your life defines when you'll reach the destination you seek. Whether you overcome them quickly or slowly, with courage or fear is up to you.

Challenges are obstacles that present themselves on your path. They can come in the form of doubts, fears, and also environmental conditions. We do not have a choice of the challenges we face, but we do have a choice in how we face them.

If we face our challenges with courage, kindness, and empathy, for ourselves and others, we can overcome them. If we face our challenges with fear and avoidance, we will find it much harder to move through them.

Challenges only present themselves when we need

them. They help shape our lives and provide us with the choices that make us who we are. If we didn't face challenges, our lives would be comfortable, but we would not have strength or courage because we wouldn't need it. If we did not meet challenges, we would not know what it's like to succeed. Challenges and adversity make us who we are.

On the path to enlightenment, there are many challenges. Some challenges will test our resolve. Some challenges will test our path and the choices we have and will make to be on it. Sometimes work will try to deviate us from our path. Sometimes family, friends, and finances. The list goes on. You will encounter some or all of these obstacles on your journey.

If you wish to travel the path to enlightenment, the one challenge you must overcome is not letting any challenge or obstacle stop you from achieving what you wish to do. Some may deviate you for a moment, a minute, a month, but you must always come back to your purpose and your path.

You must find a job that supports you on this mission. Just as you will need family, friends, and finances to help you on your way. The path to enlightenment does not mean abandoning all that you have and know; it means you need those who are going to help you push through your obstacles, not be the obstacles on your path.

As you know, the path to enlightenment can take years and even lifetimes to fulfill. How you face the challenges that arise in your life defines when you'll reach the destination you seek. Whether you overcome them quickly or slowly, with courage or fear is up to you.

The path to enlightenment does not wait for you, just as you wait for it. It is a choice. The path is always there, and the challenges will always be there. Expect challenges, and you will overcome them. Expect an easy walk, and this path will be the greatest challenge of your entire life.

The choice is yours. The challenges are yours; how you face them is up to you.

26

GUIDANCE

Listen out for our guidance like you listen out for the wind and rain. You can hear it, faintly off in the distance. If you listen and trust, we are always there, showing you the way.

On the path to enlightenment, you will find guidance from above and below.

When you receive guidance, whether it be flashes of insight or signs from nature or otherwise, follow it. When we guide you, we are showing you the way.

The path to enlightenment is a union between you and us. Without the union, you are strolling without genuinely knowing where you are going. Enlightenment is about joining with the sky again, so that our hopes and dreams may be aligned once more.

Listen out for our guidance like you listen out for the wind and rain. You can hear it faintly off in the distance. If you listen and trust, we are always there, showing you the way.

However, sometimes, you will push against us as you will believe it is you who knows the way. Trust us when we say this is not the case. We can see the path as we are above it. We have known you your whole life. We know your successes, failures, strengths, and weaknesses. We see how far along on your journey you are and how many lifetimes you have taken this path.

Life and the path to enlightenment are the same, yet people don't see it this way. People on Earth believe they are here to be successful and that this life is the only life. It is not. Some of you have been here for many thousands of years.

Earth is like a giant school where you have all been placed to learn. The sooner you realize that the one true path on Earth is enlightenment, the sooner you can begin. The longer you waste on things that do not matter, the more time you lose. The nature of life on Earth is that it can be incredibly rewarding and move you forward mentally, spiritually, and emotionally, or you can get caught up in things like money, power, and accumulation, all of which are not real.

Therefore, when we show you the way and give you the directions to take, follow them as we are trying to help. When you hear the wind, listen to our voice. Look for signs, look for opportunities that will propel you, not ones that distract.

Sometimes we may be quiet, but at these times, we are waiting for you to learn or make a decision. We are always here, waiting, watching, and wishing for you to realize what you could do if you believed.

Life is too short and too long to get caught up in human ideas. Find your way to the path and begin. You have nothing to lose and so much to gain, but you will only understand this when you start.

27

LONGEVITY

If you choose this path, know that it will be challenging and there will be some days you wish you didn't choose it. Truth be told, the path chooses you.

On the path to enlightenment, you must be and see longevity.

You must know that the path is long; therefore, your attention and commitment to it must be long also. If you see the path as being short, you will not last the distance. If you know the path is long, then you will be ready for a long journey and are more likely to complete it.

If you tackle the path day by day, without a plan, you will run out of supplies and energy. If you plan for the path potentially taking the rest of your life or longer, you will be far more successful. If you do not prepare and commit to what the path will offer daily, you will not make it to your destination.

The path to enlightenment has many highs, lows, and everything in between. It is more hard work than fun, but it is more rewarding than a life of accumulation and illusion. Journeying on the path is having a long-term goal and committing to something that is more than a lifetime, knowing that eventually, this journey will take you back to the sky. It is the longest delay in gratification a human being can choose, therefore it is the most important.

If you choose this path, know that it will be challenging, and there will be some days you wish you didn't choose it. Truth be told, the path chooses you. Sometimes our destiny takes us to the beginning of the path and asks if we would like to take it. At that point, we have a choice. If we have guided you there, we hope you will say yes.

However, agreeing does not mean it is guaranteed that you will make it to the end. We only choose those who are most ready to take the journey and those who are closest to completing their lifetimes here on Earth. The path itself is up to you.

If you are committed, patient and kind to yourself

and others, we will guide you. If you begin on the path, and you become selfish, impatient, and unkind, the path will be a dark and lonely place for you. In this case, we would prefer you to be off the path than on as this is not a journey that strengthens the ego; it weakens it.

We understand we have not yet told you what is on the path. The reason is that we are still preparing you for what it will take. If you wish to commence the most important journey of your life, is it not essential to know what you'll need to bring?

In time, we will share the path itself. In the meantime, you need to decide if you are ready for what it will deliver, not just today, but tomorrow and in many years. If you are ready, we will continue with our preparation.

28

EGO

Show your ego love and light, and it will be lighter and more loving. Show it no attention, and it will pay you all of its attention. Suppress it, and it will fight back, uglier and more attention-seeking than before.

If I were to define the ego, I would describe it as a friend who must always win. The friend who needs accomplishment and success to know their value. The friend who needs to be the best, no matter what the cost.

Ego lies within all of us. Ego is the test here on Earth. If we can defeat and disempower the ego, then we have no-one holding us to a certain standard except ourselves.

In every human being, there is both light and darkness. The ego sits in the dark, whispering to us that we must be better. Better than who we are now and better than those around us. For the ego, it is always a race to the top of the mountain.

The ego is a hard taskmaster who is never satisfied. The little voice inside us that says, 'You're right, and everyone else is wrong.'

While the ego represents the vainer parts of human nature, it is one of the uglier parts of ourselves. If we were to say all of the traits we do not like in other people, our ego holds them all. It is the one who doesn't want to be beaten and will never accept a loss. Our ego is the one who beats us up after class if we did not receive the test score we wanted and also the one who keeps us awake at night.

What human beings must learn is the ego will never be satisfied. Ever. It is our job here to realize that, and the moment we do the pressure eases. The ego only has control if we give it control.

If we can remove the power from our egos, we can be free. There would be no standards, much less pain, and much more light. We would not judge other people for who they are and where they've come from, and we would not punish ourselves for not achieving all we said we would. We would merely pursue the goals our heart desires, versus pursuing the goals we believe society desires from us.

On Earth, in this life, we are only here for a short time. The ego punishes and pushes us unnecessarily. The earlier in our life we can learn to control our ego, the more we can enjoy our lives.

Without ego, we can only love ourselves and others. Without ego, we can do what we wish to without fear of being judged for not achieving 'enough.' Without the ego, there is no impossible ladder beckoning us to reach the top when the 'top' doesn't exist.

The ego tortures us, but we let it, and as long as we let it, it will have power over us, our decisions, our happiness, and our lives. As you are aware, though, we cannot have light without darkness, and losing our ego would mean we are enlightened. Therefore, let us not speak of no ego; let us talk about maintaining our ego instead.

If you wish to maintain your ego and 'keep it in check,' do not let it run your life. You are the only person who can do that. When the ego gives you a hard time for not winning, ask it why it is essential to win and teach it that winning isn't everything.

Think of the ego as a being that remains almost always in a childlike state. Therefore, to maintain the ego, we must teach it to be kinder to ourselves and others. We must teach it to think before it speaks and not to judge others. The ego, like a human being, can be kinder or harsher depending on the love we give it.

Show your ego love and light, and it will be lighter and more loving. Show it no attention, and it will pay you all of its attention. Suppress it, and it will fight back, uglier, and more attention-seeking than before.

The ego must be managed, cared for, and taught like a child going through the 'terrible twos.' If you can persist, you will be able to anticipate its moves before it acts. You will know its weak points so you can work on them ahead of time. In doing this, we are not appeasing the ego, we are learning what powers it, and by determining what powers it, we can remove its power.

The ego is what pushes us, but it can also be what pulls us down.

Do not pretend it is not there, as it will work harder to prove to you that it is. Instead, seek to manage it, cooperate with it, and through doing so, you will be back in control of your destiny.

The path to enlightenment is not easy, and the ego will try to lead you down the wrong path every time. The only way you'll see the right path is if you can quiet the ego long enough to be able to look. The ego will do everything it can to derail your journey in a bid to save itself because, ultimately, enlightenment means the ceasing of the ego.

The ego is a bad-tempered and competitive gatekeeper who will stand in your way. Instead of pushing against it, engage with it, teach and negotiate with it, and the path will begin to open up, but do not take it with you unless you wish for your journey to be harder. Know it will need to check in with you now and again, but do not agree to any terms and conditions as the path to enlightenment holds no terms and conditions. It is what it is.

29

MOLECULES

You are no more than and no less than molecules, as is every other living being here on Earth.

Billions of molecules are what make up your earthly body. You are the sum of them, but you are also nothing at all. If you look at the body only as molecules, then that will be how you see the body, without the ego. If you look at the body as the body, then the ego is present.

When we are just molecules, we are like every other animal, plant, or human being on Earth. There is no difference other than how the molecules are made up. When we view ourselves as a body, we perceive ourselves to be greater than other creatures who are also made of molecules.

You are no more than and no less than molecules,

as is every other living being here on Earth. The shapes, sizes, and forms these molecules make will change, but at our essence, we are all the same.

Do not fall for the trick of the body, as the body does not exist. Do not fall for the trap of thinking humans are a superior species as you are not. You are equal to all others and always have been. Do not fall for the idea that all life comes from you, and all life will continue to be controlled by human hands. While you are the farmer now, there is every chance you may be farmed in the future.

Look at the body as only molecules, and you will only see molecules. Look at yourself as the body, and you will see the ego and the control that all human beings crave. We are what we perceive ourselves to be, and this is our choice.

See your choice, see the possibilities of looking at the world in a new way and see all that you are and all that you know. Know that your views can change daily, like the wind. Change is possible for all of us, no matter how far we have ventured down one path or another.

You have permission to change just as you have permission to see yourself and others beyond the form you see now. The body does not make the man, the mind, and the soul makes the man. Human beings have had a good run on Earth, but do not assume that this will continue in the way that it has. Power on Earth comes and goes. In the scope of time, human beings have been here for such a small amount of it. Do not let arrogance blind your way. Do not allow power to take hold of your soul. Do not let ego show you the way as the ego's purpose on Earth is to distract.

Start living now as you would do if you had always seen yourself and others as only molecules, and the world will change for you. Continue to live as you always have, and you will remain lost in an illusion. The choice is yours.

30

EXPECTATIONS

Life is too short and too long not to know what binds you and what is worth being bound for.

When we have expectations, we are setting a certain level for ourselves and others to meet. When they or we do not reach that level, we are disappointed. What we must realize is there are many reasons why that meeting of standards did not occur. It could be time, fatigue, money, relationships, or any number of different things.

What we must contemplate is whether our expectations of others and ourselves is realistic, given the pressures we are all under. We are each trying to do the best we can, and generally, through no fault of our own, we fail at many things, not because we don't have a desire to complete them, but because there are too many expectations to meet.

Ask yourself if the expectations you are trying to reach or asking others to meet are realistic for the volume of expectations you have. Ask yourself if your expectations are necessary or just nice to have. Often the expectations we create in our mind in times of stress are a way of protecting ourselves. Some we need and some we don't.

If we are to do anything around our expectations, it must be continually assessing if they are just or unjust, for control or to be controlling. There are particular standards we must live to yes, but when we feel out of control, we often try to control others and the world around us.

We are each responsible for ourselves, and each of us must define the expectations we are willing to meet. Some are needed, some are not, and it is only you who must decide which expectations you will abide by and which you won't. If you struggle to see which is which, ask yourself if each expectation is right or binding for you? Are the expectations someone else has put on you healthy or unhealthy?

If you are to understand the difference, you must

look at each one individually. For those that don't matter or don't align with who you are, what you want, and the type of person you wish to be shed them. For those that do matter, to yourself and others, work to meet them as this is an agreement you made.

Life is built on relationships, and relationships can either be healthy or unhealthy. Our relationships are made up of expectations, some healthy, some not. Decide which are worth keeping and which are not. Know that you have a choice, even when you feel you do not.

Life is too short and too long not to know what binds you and what is worth being bound for. Your life and how you live it is always your decision. We are merely here to guide you and shed light on the things that otherwise may have been left in the darkness.

31

GRANDEUR

When we choose grandeur over wisdom and knowledge, we choose objects that live and die with us, never being more than what they were created to be.

We do not need grandeur in our lives to feel good about what we have created. Our lives are not measured by what we collect, but by what we create.

If we create a good life and we choose substance over grandeur, we will be rewarded with gifts that only the soul can receive. If we want grandeur over substance, we will collect objects we cannot take with us from this life to the next. When we choose grandeur over wisdom and knowledge, we choose objects that live and die with us, never being more than what they were created to be.

Our lives here on Earth are so much more important than what we perceive them to be. We have an opportunity to make a difference here to friends, family, and all the people of the world, yet often, we choose a life of accumulation over a lifetime of giving. If you can create a life where you are giving, you will also receive. If you create a life where you continuously take, then all will be taken from you when you die.

The most important gift we can give ourselves and others is love and kindness. Without these, the world is hollow and empty. In time the world will come to learn that life is not made by what we take, but by what we give. It is as we become older that we realize the sum of our actions creates the life we have, whether we are satisfied with it or not.

In times of struggle, we cannot seek comfort from the objects around us, but from the people we have invested in. In times of pain or sickness, an object will not make us better or healthier, but love will. When we need belief in ourselves or others, objects cannot give us what love will.

Love is boundless, love is free, and love is what we all need to survive and flourish. If we do not have love and gratitude, we have nothing. Just as the wind can have tremendous power or be nothing at all, we are the same. Just as time can give, it can also taketh away.

Know that grandeur will only satisfy you temporarily. Know your life is not what you collect, but what you give. Grandeur does not provide warmth, kindness, or love; grandeur fills a space left empty by all that is missing.

Life can be as full or as empty as we make it, but make it full of what you can take with you and all that cannot be taken from you, and you will lead a happy life.

32

CLARITY

When you do not commit to one path, you can remain standing in the forest for all of eternity.

Only when you are clear will you know the way forward, and only when you know the way forward will you be able to move.

Currently, you are in a forest, and you are not aware of the way. You sense one direction is better than another, but you have not yet committed to one particular path, the right path. When you do not commit to one path, you can remain standing in the forest for all of eternity. Taking a few steps forward, and a few steps back does not constitute committing to a path. It means trying a path, getting scared, and turning back.

There have been times when you have committed

to a path, and it has felt good, but then events or situations have scared you back into your comfort zone. What you must realize about the forest is that if you do not choose a path, you can stay there forever, never choosing anything. It is only through selecting a path that you will gain clarity, and only through clarity can you move forward.

Which path will you choose? Will you choose the path back to your old life and old self, or will you choose the path to the self you do not know yet? Indecision is dragging you down like a weight in the ocean, never knowing the true depths of how far down you can go.

If you embrace the new path to the new you, you will find that life will simplify itself. The people who are part of your old life who need to fall away will fall away, just like the jobs and friends who need to fall away will do the same.

Choosing the new path or the old path sets events in motion to support that choice. If you're ready to pursue the new you, then make your decision. If you're not comfortable and you wish to return to the old you, you may do this also. We will not stop you. If you need more time to decide, then please, by all means, stay in the forest and spend more time choosing between the new and the old you.

We know which path you should choose, as do you, but you must have the courage and conviction to stand in your decision. As you are in the forest alone, no-one can push you onto the new or old path but you.

Isn't it time you made a decision?

Perhaps time will help, but maybe it won't. Perhaps it's embracing your true destiny, the one that scares you that is the right choice.

Only you can choose the way, and only you can decide when is the right time. Please remember, however, that the longer you stand in the forest, the less time you have to do what you need to do. Make a decision, and the rest will fall into place. Trust us on this. Life does not come to you, you must go to it, but first, you must choose.

33

NEGLECT

If a bird cannot sing, it is no longer a bird. If you do not allow your soul to sing its true song, then life on Earth can feel empty.

When we neglect our dreams, we become empty.

When we forget what we've always dreamed of doing, or we choose responsibility instead of enjoyment and what our heart desires, we will never feel full. Money, power, or fame will never fill us up, even if we have all of those objects at the same time.

It is not whether you are rich or poor that defines how much you enjoy life; it is whether you are pursuing what your heart truly desires. If a bird cannot sing, it is no longer a bird. If you do not allow your soul to sing its true song, then life on Earth can feel empty.

In our lives, the greatest thing we can do is love others and love ourselves. We do not love ourselves when we give up all that we dream of to fit in. We do not love ourselves when we sacrifice who we are for a world that celebrates conformity, as even those who appear not to conform are always doing so in some way.

What we must realize is that fulfilling our soul's mission while we are here is our only real goal. If we cannot do this, we have failed our mission, our purpose, our song. All that we ask you to do is try. Try to be bigger than what you would usually allow yourself to be. Try to be more than you think or know is possible. Try to let more love to come into your heart, more than you know is possible.

Try to expel fear and not fall for the tricks of humanity and a world that acts like a big army walking towards one destination. Know that if you choose to leave the defined path, you are walking closer to us. Know that by leaving the defined path, you are showing others they can do the same, even if they do not commit to it out loud. It is through our actions that we inspire others and the world does not become any greater by us playing small.

When we pass away, it is not what we did do that will

surround us in the next life; it is what we did not do. If you live a half-life in this life, you will remember this half-life in your next. If you lived a full life and tried the best you could to do more, be more, and show others they can do the same; the sky is the limit in your next life.

Enjoy your time here. No amount of responsibility is worth more than your soul singing. Fighting to suppress your song only damages you and excites those who wish for you to be no more than them.

Surround yourself with people who want you to do more, be more, and show more and you will lift them up too. Life is to be filled, fully, wholeheartedly, and with more joy and wisdom than you ever thought possible. Enjoy this life, and enjoy tomorrow. You deserve it.

34

BRAVERY

When you think of bravery, think about how water breaks new ground. Rivers are not born in a day; they are created over time. It is the same with bravery.

When we are brave, we are strong and purposeful, despite anything in our environment that may be working against us being so. When we are brave, we can accomplish anything. There is no wall too high and no bridge too long. Even when there are breaks in the bridge, there is nothing that will stop us from moving across it.

Bravery is needed in all parts of our lives, in our relationships, in our work, and at play. Bravery adds an element that no other quality or characteristic in our lives can add as it pushes us further. Without bravery, we would not accomplish our dreams, our mission, or our purpose.

To be brave, one must know that what they are working towards is worthwhile. To be brave, one must step into the unknown and know that whatever is there is right at this point.

Without bravery, we are lost, stuck in a never-ending circle of comfort. While comfort is sweet for the soul, it does not help the soul grow as much as it could.

Take what you know of bravery and expand it into something new and bigger. Ask yourself what you need or want to be brave for and figure out how to do that. Ask yourself why you need to be brave and confirm it is something you want.

The waterfall plunges over the edge of the cliff only when it is ready. In the beginning, it starts as a trickle and grows into a strong and powerful surge of water so undeniably strong that no-one would get in its way. Bravery begins with the tiniest of trickles and develops into a strong and powerful wave.

When you think of bravery, think about how water breaks new ground. Rivers are not born in a day;

they are created over time. It is the same with bravery.

Begin your trickle, and you too will eventually turn into a wave.

35

CHANGE

Life changes as quickly as sand moves through an hourglass. The choice you have is what you do with that time because it will pass you by anyway.

When we are ready for change, change will come. Although sometimes, when we are not ready for it, change will also come as this is the nature of change. Change happens when we are both prepared and unprepared for it.If you were to look at your life as an hourglass, you would recognize how much time has already passed — the sands of time shift whether you wish for them to or not. How quickly time flies or does not fly is not up to you. What you do have is the time that has been given to you to achieve what you've been born to do.

If you accept what you've been born to do, you've

lost the time that's already passed by to do it. All the time you have left is what's in the hourglass. The challenge is you don't know how much sand is gone; you only know that sand exists. Life changes as quickly as the sand moves through the hourglass. The choice you have is what you do with that time because it's passing you by anyway.

If you do not use your time wisely and to your highest good, the time you have left will not be time you can be proud of. If you do use your time for your highest good, then you can move towards fulfilling your purpose here on Earth.

What you must realize is what lies outside of this purpose is change. Change takes you closer to your purpose, and change can also alter your purpose. What you believe your purpose to be now will likely change in ten years. All you can do is move towards the purpose you see for yourself right now.

What you must know is that your purpose is not wrapped up in things or achievements. Your purpose is not a job, a lifestyle, or finding a way to make life here on Earth more comfortable. Your purpose is to serve the Earth. All of our purposes are to help the Earth, her people, plants, and animals.

Our purpose is to assist in the community of life. Not just in the city you live in, but in the broader community of life on Earth. The Earth needs helpers, and we have all been brought here to help.

By furthering our own ways and means, we are not helping the Earth; we are helping ourselves. By helping ourselves, we are making our lives here less meaningful than what they could be if we helped others.

When we say this, we do not speak of going and working for a charity, although some people might. What we speak of is using your skills and gifts to better the experience of life on Earth.

How can you use the gifts you have been given, not just to preserve the Earth, but to grow it? When we speak of growth, know that we do not mean adding more 'things.' We want you to help us take Earth to a new place of abundance and health.

The Earth is like a plant we have been tasked with caring for. The current state of the Earth is reflective of the fact that we always take from it and never give back. With this attitude and way of thinking, this can only go on for so long before we lose the home we have loved and created.

Think of the life you have now and how you could change it to bring more growth to the Earth. Know that change will come for you anyway, so choose how you would like to contribute. Life holds more meaning for us when we give ourselves wholly and completely.

The sands of time have shifted for you even as you have read this chapter. Do not waste time on what you do not love. Take these thoughts and integrate them with your mind, then create a plan of action. Life is too short and too long to do nothing. Make it your mission to do more, change more, see more, and be more, and both you and the Earth will be rewarded.

36

DIVINE INTERVENTION

More often than not, us entering your life is more of a wakeup call than a pleasantry.

We are all divine creatures, but sometimes we forget this when the lights and action of our earthly lives become too distracting.

All of you have free will, and free will means you are in charge of your destiny. There are some of you we have chosen to do divine tasks here on Earth, and chances are if you are reading this book, you are one of these people. We are just waiting for you to open your eyes and ears wide enough for us to show you.

Occasionally, we feel the need to step in and intervene. Sometimes you may be on a path you're not supposed to be on. Sometimes you may have drifted off somewhere to a place that is taking up more of your time than you wish to give.

When we step in, it may be pleasant or unpleasant, depending on how much we need to re-direct you back onto your path. If it is unpleasant, it may result in the loss of a job, relationship, or career. If it is pleasant, we may present gifts to entice you back onto the path.

More often than not, us entering your life is more of a wakeup call than a pleasantry. During these times, it is essential to remember that you are not alone. We are just stripping something from your life that is no longer needed or potentially wanted. You've just needed a little help or push in the right direction.

Sometimes like toddlers, we become distracted by something, and we chase it, often to our detriment. Almost always, we let you run, but only for long enough to feel like you have done what you need to, and then we guide you back.

If you are struggling to hold onto something that is no longer yours, ask yourself why.' Why am I trying so hard to hold onto this? Is its time in my life over?'

If the feeling you have is yes, its time is over, let it go. You do yourself no favors by trying to hold onto something that's no longer yours. And the longer you do hold onto it, the smaller the window for change, and the harder it is for us to introduce you to the next part of your journey.

In other words, you cannot see the new door if you do not close the old one. What's important to remember is that when you close the old door, there will be a period of darkness where you cannot see the new one. Sit with this, do not be afraid and know that the new door will appear. You just need to give yourself enough time to let go of the old door's handle to be able and ready to walk through a new one.

Life is full of old doors closing and new doors opening. See this constant change, and you will do well. Think that there are only a few doors in your life, and you will spend more time struggling to preserve old doors that no longer exist than you will be opening new ones that are better for you.

Life is full of lessons like this, and this is what we are trying to teach you. Close the old door, and the moment of darkness will be scary but exhilarating. Once the door is closed, you will see a crack of light under a new door, and this is the one you will walk toward. We will wait for you there.

MASTERY OF SELF

As the ego falls away, the guidance we provide ourselves and others will transform into pure love, without attachment, without ego and without control, which is what we wish for you and all human beings on Earth.

Before we master ourselves, we are wild, untamed beasts that cannot be contained. We believe we know the way, but everything we know is just an illusion. We try to keep our emotions contained in the world we live in.

However, when pain and fear arrives, this is when we crumble. When we feel out of control, this is when we are most likely to lash out at ourselves and others.

If we are to have mastery of self, we must treat ourselves and others with love and care at all times. We are not measured by how well we cope with typical day-to-day life, but how we deal in a crisis. When we are in crisis is when the most unattractive parts of our personality and character are revealed.

To gain mastery of self is a skill and one we must practice daily. You hear of taking the high road, and this is the road you must take. However, what this means is letting go of attachments to outcomes in your life.

Our self-mastery is tested when we feel the need to step in and regain control of a person or situation. It may be we've seen something up ahead, or we do not trust ourselves or someone else to be safe in seeing something through. Perhaps it might be an issue of reputation, bad judgement, or an issue of safety. These are all your self-perceived ideas, generally driven by the ego. When the ego is in control, we will always seek to control every situation, person, or experience in our lives.

Self-mastery is not abandoning care for the life you live or the people who live within it. It is providing guidance and not being attached to any outcome, as when the result arrives, it will be right for that person and their experience. Self-mastery is not abandonment. It is pure love and letting go. It allows you to focus on mastering yourself, as no-one will do this for you.

Imagine how much less stress you would have in your life if you could abandon the need to control everything and everyone? Even when control is dressed up as guidance, the ego is in charge.

As the ego falls away, the guidance we can provide ourselves and others will transform into pure love, without attachment, without ego and without control, which is what we wish for you and all human beings on Earth.

38

LETTING GO

Weigh up the story you've created about yourself. Weigh up the impact it's had on your life and the value it still holds. All stories on Earth are great, but sometimes new stories need to be told.

There is a difference between shedding and letting go. If shedding is the act of losing the elements in our life that are not serving us, then letting go is letting go of our former self.

All of our identity on Earth is wrapped up in things: objects, stories, jobs, and relationships. When those elements are taken away, and we have gone through the process of shedding, we are left with only our self. At this point, there is nothing of the former life left: nothing to be known by and nothing to shout or talk about. At this moment, the ego strives to regain control and re-build what has been lost or shed. It is here you must persist, saying no to the ego and demanding time to sit in the emptiness you have created. It is only through having no distractions we can see who we truly are and let go of the human identity we have created. Because while you can let all of your possessions go, you can still speak of yourself in the same way, and stories are stronger than objects. Stories change the world; objects enhance the world.

When you have shed everything which needs to be shed, you can sit with your own story without distraction.

Weigh up the story you've created about yourself. Weigh up the impact it has had on your life and the value it still holds. All stories on Earth are great, but sometimes new stories need to be told. Sometimes everything must be taken away for you to create a new story. Eventually, when you are ready, you will realize it is not the story that counts but the spirit of who you are that does.

When we move from one chapter to another, having a new story allows us to move more seamlessly between one path and another. Having no story makes it harder because human beings are naturally suspicious. Having a story means people are less likely to ask questions about your ongoing journey.

We are not suggesting you lie. We are explaining a simple human truth. People like stories, and having a story that allows you to transition from one path to another will make your journey easier. You do not want people standing in your way. In your mind, know where you are heading. The story is simply the cover of a book that has not yet been written.

Many people are moving towards more spiritual paths, but it is creating a lot of suspicion on Earth. Human beings can only deal with what they can see, which is interesting because the nature of religion means investing yourself in something unseen. What you will notice humans are clinging to is the bible, which is a story. People can deal with change and with the unknown if there is a story to refer back to.

In your life, as you change and evolve, having a story is not for the benefit of you; it is in the interest of others to make your life easier. One day we will live in a time where humans can speak their complete truth, but that time is not now.

It is important to have a story and one that other

people can relate to. The reason it's important is that it allows you the time and space to let go of the identity you've created and held onto so tightly. The story holds the space while you do important work on yourself.

In time, you can shed the story as you will have had the time to know who you are at this point in your journey. Who you are will continue to change as life goes on.

In your life, you will shed many people, jobs, objects, relationships, and experiences. After you have shed, reflect on the identity you have created and sit in the emptiness for a time until you are ready to move forward again. Know this is ok, that it is pre-destined and that your story is important, so you have the space to receive your next steps.

Life is a great spiritual adventure interrupted by our ego and other human beings. Give other people what they want and give the ego what it needs, which is to be put back into its box for a time so you can work untethered by its objectives.

In time, you will grow to love shedding as it will come as frequently as the seasons on Earth change. The more you can shed and reflect, the more you can become who you really are, which is a glorious and divine creature who has come to Earth to learn.

When you know who you are, you can learn to let go and realize that what you do was never what was most important about your birth and your birth rite.

39

PROMISES

Sometimes we make promises to ourselves we should never have made.

When you make a promise to yourself or others, you are expected to keep it. When the promise is one you cannot keep, it is best to confront the issue head-on.

The reasons you may not be able to keep a promise are many. You may have had a change of heart or never wished for that outcome in the first place, yet you felt you had to keep or make the promise to keep someone or something in your life.

Sometimes we make promises to ourselves we should never have made. These promises might be to love someone forever or to keep progressing along a particular career path. The challenge with something like this is you have made a promise to yourself, which can make it easier to resolve, but also harder.

The reason it is harder is that we tend to hold ourselves to goals and expectations we know we cannot or should not meet. Sometimes we make rushed decisions or decisions we feel are right at the time, only to discover the decisions we made were never what we wanted at all. Sometimes we make decisions because we think it will make someone else happy.

What we must uncover and assess are the promises we've made to ourselves and others. What we must weigh up is are those promises worth keeping and those worth resolving and letting go.

Unfulfilled promises hang in the air like clouds in the sky. Even when it is the night time, you still know they're there. If you can fulfill or resolve them, they'll disappear.

When we make promises we can't keep, it damages our soul, because our mind and body tell us in advance that we won't be able to keep these promises which degrades our truth and our integrity.

If you wish to make promises, you may, but consider their implications in the long term, long after the shine has come off the course you finished, the promotion you took, or the relationship you promised would last for eternity.

Some might say it's easier not to make promises. Some might say it's easier to make them. What we know and what you must consider is that not all promises are made equal, and not all of them are intended to be forever. Some promises drive us for a lifetime, and some promises pass us by as quickly as the wind passes over water. The challenge for human beings is it's often hard to know the difference. All we ask is that when you make a promise, you make it for the right reasons.

Know that some promises should never be made, as while you feel one way now, you may not feel that way in the future.

Remember that the promises we make in our lives hang over our heads like the clouds in the sky. Unresolved promises add up and take a toll across all parts of our life. And making too many promises and seeing them through can take up all of our life, leaving no time to do what you were brought here to do. It is wise to know promises as well as you know yourself.

40

MONEY: PART 2

Money is not the answer; it is a hindrance. Trading empowers people to give from the heart and return to spirit and their purpose here on Earth.

When you are earning money, you can buy the things you need and want. When you're not earning money, you can't. When we live in a society driven by money, it makes it difficult for those who aren't to survive as their values are misaligned.

If we were to take away all of the world's money, the world would be in chaos for a time, and then we would learn to trade again. Except we would trade based on our strengths, not what we have been paid to do in the past.

The challenge for human beings is the things we love are often not the things that pay our bills on

Earth, which is a shame because, in our hearts, we are makers. We were born to make things, yet large factories produce everything here on Earth. What this means is that the makers can no longer afford to make what we need as a job.

If we lived in a world where we were trading our strengths and unique abilities for what we needed, the world would have more equality. Currently, most of the Earth's population work in jobs they don't enjoy, which means we have forgotten who we are.

If the world had no money and no financial structure, you would trade your abilities with those who had what you needed. If you needed food, you would offer your gifts in exchange for food. If you required furniture or teaching, you would exchange your skills and abilities for the furniture you wanted and the lessons you needed. The world would be far more straightforward.

In our hearts, we all need something. Often we lose track of what that something is though, because it has become covered up by money. We no longer look directly at what we need; we look at what we want, which is money.

We believe money opens up our options, but really, it closes them down. If we were smart, we would go back to doing what we once did before money was invented, as money rewards the rich and takes from the poor. Before money, we all had skills to trade, and everything was equal, which is the way of life we must go back to. Money can still play a part, but it cannot be the only currency.

Offering our skills in exchange for the services we need is about encouraging ourselves and others to go back to what they are good at, which in turn will help them find their joy. To begin it is simple, figure out what you need and explain what you will give in return. This practice is the way and the way back to who we were and who we can become.

Money is not the answer; it is a hindrance. Trading empowers people to give from the heart and return to spirit and their purpose here on Earth. Take this into consideration.

41

CHANNELING

Watch and listen for the signs we are showing you that you are on the right or wrong path, as they are always there.

When you are aware and awake, you can channel guidance from the universe. Everything you ever needed or wanted to know is there waiting for you.

When we speak of channeling, we do not speak of it in the traditional sense. We speak of it as asking you to look for signs that we are communicating with you. These signs can be from nature, through numbers and things you can feel, see, or hear. We are a presence that is always with you, even when you think we are not.

Life presents us with many challenges, and the awakening process is one of them. During your awakening, you will feel out of sorts, and like you no longer fit in the world you've created. These feelings are normal as what awakening does is disconnect you from the world you've created so you may find the world we wish to connect you with. This will not be easy. There will friends, family, and relationships lost along the way. It is not a road for the lighthearted, nor would the lighthearted want this journey.

What we can assure you is that this feeling of disconnection won't last long in the scheme of your life. It will only be a period where you no longer identify with the you that came before and what that version of you created.

The friends, family, and jobs that are right for you will remain. The rest will fall away as they weigh you down. Much like an anchor secures the ship in the harbor, those who do not see the real you will only slow down your progress. Therefore, release these people and roles in the kindest way possible as they served you at a time when you needed it most. Now you need something different.

When you're ready, you will find new people or roles that will suit you better, and you will find that life will show you the way. Watch and listen for the signs we're showing you that you are on the right or wrong path, as they are always there. We are always there.

42

MANAGING YOUR TIME

The way to become happier is to live with only what you need and to spend your time and energy with those who need it most.

When you are managing your time, you have time for everything and everyone important. When you are not managing your time, you do not.

Every human being on Earth is obsessed with the management of time, but what is the point of managing time when all of your time is consumed doing what you do not love? What is the point of managing your time when you spend all of your time doing a job, and very little time on finding and pursuing your higher purpose?

We understand you need to make an income, and we know how the world works because we made it. However, we cannot help you when you do not help us. We cannot bring you joy when you get caught up in human games, like pursuing a career that drains all of your time.

The time you are here for in this body is already so limited, and even if you were to live to one-hundred, you wouldn't accomplish all that you could, yet most of us do not get anywhere near this age. Most of us spend our whole lives chasing something that does not exist. Most of us know we're wasting our time, but we don't know how to stop. The wheel of time keeps spinning as we try to become more efficient, but even then, we continue to waste more time.

The problem is not time, nor is it how efficient we are with using our time. Our problem is we spend most of our time on the wrong things. We spend our time in jobs we don't enjoy to earn money and spend it on objects we don't need. We try to compete with others to measure our success. We waste the years of our children's lives chasing freedom when all we create is more slavery.

There is an answer to how we beat time, and that is by dedicating your time to the people you love, the lessons you want to learn here on Earth, and by giving back.

You may think, 'I can't do those things, we'll starve!'. To which we say, 'No, you will not.' The positive energy you create by giving back to the Earth and concentrating on your real purpose here will lead you to more abundance than you ever dreamed possible.

The real purpose of being on Earth is to learn your karmic lessons and to keep proceeding with them, life by life. When you waste your time on other things, you will keep coming back to learn what you could have done in one lifetime, but because of humanity's obsession with accumulation and success, it takes ten lifetimes. This is how human beings spend their time, and this is how we continue to get it wrong again and again. This is why we are all so unhappy, yet we assume that by accumulating more, we will be even happier. This is not the way.

The way to become happier is to live with only what you need so you can spend your time and energy with those who need it most. We were all born with skills that allow us to give back to the planet, but we do not use them. We have gifts that we've been given, yet we put them aside for an 'office job.'

If you can look at time as something that slips by, you would use it more productively. If you can look at the world not through the eyes of accumulation, but through how to create more peace and love, your time here would be more valuable.

Life is to be lived, yet we spend so much time not living at all. Break free, break the mold, and don't be afraid to do it as you always have our support, guidance, love, and we will never let you down. Take this advice and give yourself time to think about it, as time spent thinking about time will provide you with a new lease on life.

43

HOME

Your home is your temple and only invite those into your home who work for yours and their highest good.

Your home is your temple. It is the place you own where you deem yourself to be safe. It is your refuge and a place to curate your little piece of the world.

When you invite people into your home, you are inviting in other energies. Some are good, and some are bad. Rather than welcoming everybody in, treat your home as a sacred space where only good energies are invited. We understand this may present some obstacles, especially when it comes to family and friends. Nonetheless, we ask that you do what you can to keep the energy in your home as protected as possible from all who may seek to consume or harm it.

If you think of your home as a sacred space, with all of your energy contained inside, it becomes easier to imagine who you wish to invite in and who you would prefer to meet in a different location.

Human beings today are very unaware of energy and will invite anyone into their home, believing it to be just four walls and a roof, but it is not. It is an energetic hub. Where light brings more light, darkness invited into a sacred space can arrive and never leave. Therefore, when considering inviting a person or energy into your home, ask yourself, 'Is this person or energy worthy of coming into my sacred space? Is their energy pure and light? Are their actions filled with good intentions?'.

What can be challenging for human beings new to the spiritual space is that some darker beings or energies may mask themselves in light, which can be intentional or unintentional. To provide an example, human beings driven by money, fame, and power tend to be motivated by darker energies, even if they perceive it to be light. What must be realized is that light energy is selfless and not driven by accumulation. Money, power, and consumption drive darkness. It is here we find the difference. Other darker energies you may experience in people include jealousy. Jealousy is driven by a darker force, just as being competitive is driven by darker forces, because the nature and aim of these emotions are to separate, not bring human beings together.

We all have varying levels of darkness within us. However, some humans are naturally darker in their energy, and some are naturally lighter. What we are suggesting is that you consider who you invite into your home and to question what their intentions are. It takes time to build light energy in a home, and it would be a shame to let darker energies in to consume the light you have created.

If you are unsure if someone you know is light or dark, then it is safer for all to meet in a different space. Your home is your temple and only invite those into your home who work for yours and their highest good. Remember that your home is alive with energy, and the balance of this energy takes time to change.

Care for your home and its energy like it is a sacred space. If you own a smudge stick containing white sage, it is best to move through your home at least once a week to ward off and clear any darker energies. Burn candles to create more light. Keep your home clean and tidy, leaving no dark corners or mess for energies to hide in or stagnate.

Think of your home as a temple, treat it like a temple, and only invite those who offer goodness to your temple. All others may be met in a different space.

44

PROGRESS

Progress makes the soul feel lighter and freer.

When you are making progress, you are moving in the right direction, and this is something you can feel. It is like the gates have opened, and light is streaming through. Progress makes the soul feel lighter and freer.

For us to make progress, we must listen to what our guides and intuition have to say and move in that guided direction, even if what is being put forward seems unusual. The only way to progress is to trust and not to move in the ways we already know, but in the ways we do not know.

In our lives on Earth, there are the well-trodden paths, and then there are those that are not paths yet. This is the direction you must take, as the answers you are seeking cannot be found on well-trodden paths. They'll be found in the wilderness, where the environment is quiet and untainted by the sound of many footsteps. In remote locations where the stars can easily be seen and followed, because there is no pollution in the sky. And in places where you can be truly alone and give yourself time and space to think.

On well-trodden paths, there is too much noise and disturbance. People talk, and you cannot hear the sounds of nature. The route is busy, and you can't see what's ahead. All you can see are the feet in front of you.

No-one finds the answers they are looking for on the well-trodden paths. You will find other people, but not answers. If you are looking for company, you will find it, but if you are looking for solitude, space, and a new direction, you have come to the wrong place.

If you wish to make progress, you must veer off the path and into the night, to places where the sky is brighter and the sounds much quieter. It is out in the wilderness that you'll hear your guides and intuition speaking to you, softly, urging you to keep going.

If what you wish for is to find the path to

enlightenment, you will find it by creating it yourself. It is not a path you can make your way to, and it is not signposted because it does not exist. It is of your creation, as every path to enlightenment is different and unique to the individual.

What you must understand is that by staying on the path well-trodden, you will never go anywhere. It is an illusion and a trick. What we yearn for you to realize is all that what you're seeking does not lie on this path; it lies off it. If you can recognize this, the way forward becomes lighter and more apparent. There will be dark nights, but there are dark nights on well-trodden paths too. At least by treading your way, you can discover yourself and not others.

Life is a big adventure, but by taking the same road as everybody else, we are not partaking in an adventure, we are participating in drudgery. Walk off the path, and you will be rewarded. Keep walking forward, and even on the darkest of nights, you will see progress.

45

MOMENTUM

It is movement that sets us free and stagnation that weighs us down. If there is time to sit and stagnate, there is time to move, and this is what we wish you to do.

When you have momentum, you are consistently gaining pace. Momentum is the driver of all significant changes in the world, as it promotes constant change.

In our lives on Earth, we can happen to Earth, or Earth can happen to us. Both have different outcomes. If we decide what we want to do with our life here, we can start moving towards accomplishing this goal. If we have not decided what we'd like to do, this does not mean we should stop; it means we must continue to move until we decide.

We must move even when we don't know where to move to, even when the idea of moving pains us. It is movement that sets us free and stagnation that weighs us down. If there is time to sit and stagnate, there is time to move, and this is what we wish you to do.

Finding your life's purpose takes time, and it is a journey to get there. The mind molds to the shape of the idea over time. If we told you what your life's purpose is, your mind might not be ready for it and not cope. It may even repel the idea as it is so far from where you are now you would question our existence and sanity.

However, if over time, you allow yourself to discover your life purpose through movement, you will come to embrace the idea on your own, which also means there is a much higher chance of you seeing it through.

If you do not know what your purpose is, if you keep moving, you will discover it in time and when your mind is ready. If you have not found it yet, then your mind may not be prepared. That does not mean that this won't change tomorrow, the day after or next month. The mind is always moving and evolving, as long as we give it the reason to do so.

Sometimes change can feel too slow. Trust us when we say that every move, even if it feels small, contributes to the greater whole and your greater movement, so on the days where you feel like doing nothing, do something. And on the days where you feel like changing the world, change it and do something bold. In the end, both big leaps and small steps equal each other out and give us momentum.

If you can create momentum and stick with it day in and day out, you will see the changes you desire to see in the world and also in yourself.

46

COMMITMENT

If you are seeking the path to enlightenment, you must make room for the path on every day of the year for the rest of your life.

When you are committed, you will reap the rewards of your hard work. When you are not committed, there may be rewards, but they will be few and far between.

The nature of commitment is that you must show you can weather both the sun and the storm. Day in and day out, you demonstrate your commitment by showing up, taking part, and learning as much as you can. If you are not committed, you will not see the real rewards that commitment can bring, which is continued growth and transformation.

There are times in our lives when we are more

committed than others. There are times in our lives when it is easier to commit than others. This is because sometimes there is a lot on for us, mentally, spiritually, and emotionally, and other times very little.

If you are seeking the path to enlightenment, you must make room for the path every day for the rest of your life. Not for a day, a week, or a month, but every day, week, and month until you arrive there or continue this journey into your next life.

If you cannot show up every day to learn and take part in our helping shape your destiny, then you should not be there. If you are willing to commit, every day and you show up every day, then your potential and the potential for rewards are limitless. You are limitless.

However, you are not limitless without hard work, resilience, courage, and strength. Without these, you will struggle to keep pushing through on the days where life expects much of you, and the path expects little. Some days the path will be quiet, whispering the question, "Will you come back today?" and some days, it will yell. On the days when it is quiet, will you hear it as it calls and will you come? When your life is loud, and the demands on you are heavy, will you still tend to the path?

These are the times you must keep going, more than when you are carefree. It is the hard days that matter, and it is the hard days we most wish to see you there, turning up with your hiking pack and your shoes, ready for the next part of the journey. The path to enlightenment and your life journey may appear to be the same, but they are different. One is for those that seek to realize their full potential in the universal sense as a spirit. The other is for those who seek to understand their full potential as a human being.

If you wish to be on the path to enlightenment, you must be happy to abandon all in your life that you have built to discover all that you may become. The path is not about accumulation; it is about shedding, stripping back until you are naked, leaving yourself only with the pack on your back, the shoes on your feet, and the wisdom you have found.

It is wisdom that will take you further than you have ever been before. It is the awareness that life can take everything from you, but it cannot take your spirit that matters. It is understanding that the real jewels you seek are not outside of you; they are within you waiting to be discovered. But first, you must show up.

47

MAINTAINING THE BODY AND MIND

The ultimate goal is for you and spirit to move with each other, entirely in sync like two snakes travelling in unison.

To be able to undertake the path to enlightenment, you must maintain your body and your mind. If your body is weak and unwell, then your mind will also be weak and unwell. The mind and body are connected, and each influences the other.

If you wish to undertake the path, your body must be fit, supple, and able to move in all directions at any time. We are not expecting you to be a gymnast; however, when spirit moves through you, the more you can move with spirit, the better results you'll receive.

For this, we recommend yoga and walking. Yoga moves your body in ways it is not used to, and walking allows the body time in nature to absorb and re-balance. If you are beginning yoga, we recommend practicing Shakti Yoga. If you do not usually go out walking, then we recommend walking in nature for thirty minutes each day. If you cannot be in nature, then we recommend going out when the world is quiet. Early in the morning is best.

If you can practice yoga and work on your flexibility and also do some light exercise through walking, you will feel much better, and spirit will be able to better flow through you. The ultimate goal is for you and spirit to move with each other, entirely in sync like two snakes traveling in unison.

To keep the mind maintained, we recommend meditation. The length of your meditation is up to you, but make sure it is consistent and try to push your mind to go further each time. The challenge with our minds, especially in the Western world, is that they are so busy. To only meditate for five or ten minutes does not allow the mind to shed what it is currently working through. It is when we have enough time to free the mind and meditate on top of that, that meditation becomes truly valuable.

If the time you meditate for is too short, you are merely meditating based on what is already in your mind. Take the time to empty it, and then do five to ten minutes on top of that. Twenty minutes is an excellent place to start.

Begin with walking, Shakti Yoga, and meditation.

48

HEALTH

We may be eternal in spirit, but our body here on Earth remains our most significant limitation.

As you awaken, your health may suffer.

Many people assume that those who are the most spiritual are the healthiest, which is not always the case. Some people experience awakening symptoms that create disharmony in the body. Sometimes to find harmony, we must experience disharmony first.

Those who are awakening may experience sickness, energetic disturbances, aches and pains, and an overall feeling of lethargy, which is normal as your body awakens to its more spiritual center. What we ask you to do during these times is allow more time for rest and recuperation. We understand that you have lives to take care of; however, it is our job to look after your life, and we ask you to rest if needed.

There may be times when your awakening symptoms make more sense than others. Sometimes it may be harder than easier to embrace who you are in a spiritual and physical form. We promise that this relationship will change over time. If you are experiencing symptoms that are not in line with how you usually feel, we suggest keeping an eye on this. When the energies of our other dimensional selves merge with the physical self in this plane, it can cause the body to jar and act in ways that seem out of character.

Where the body is usually calm and smooth in its movements, in the awakening process, you may find it jolts or is subject to fatigue, aches, and unexplainable pains. Sit with this, ride it out, but if it continues to cause concern, please see someone who can allay your fears. Where some symptoms are caused by the nature of our body and mind spiritually awakening, sometimes there are more in-depth causes that must be investigated. We may be eternal in spirit, but our physical body remains our most significant limitation.

We ask that you give yourself enough sleep, water,

and nutrients to carry the body through this process, no matter how long it takes. The path to enlightenment is not something done over a day or a decade. It will most likely even continue in our death, where we will work on our path to ascension as much as we did in our life.

HOPE: PART 2

When we feel like we've lost our way, it is hope that helps us find our way back.

When the darkest of nights fall, and we can no longer see the sun, it is hope that lights up the night. When we are cold, and we feel there is nothing to keep us warm, it is hope that wraps itself around us. When we feel like we've lost our way, it is hope that helps us find our way back. Without hope, we are hopeless. Without a dream to chase, we are dreamless. Without love in our lives, we are loveless.

When we have hope, even in the smallest of things, we can build this hope to become bigger. When we have a dream, even the smallest of them, with hope, we can dream a little bigger. When we have love in our lives, love can bring with it both our hopes and our dreams.

If we spend too much of our time facing reality, we will put all of our hopes and our dreams aside because reality does not allow for hopes and dreams. If we allow reality to take over, committing ourselves to life in a job we no longer enjoy, hope can be taken as swiftly as it arrives. Do not aim to live without hope, as it will be a fruitless life in every sense of the word. Even when it seems like we are moving further away from our goals if we have hope we can quickly find our way back. Reality is the enemy of hope as reality always tries to bring us back down to Earth, and it is always trying to tell us what is and isn't realistic. No-one has the right or the knowledge to tell you what is realistic and what is not.

If you listen to reality and become too consumed by it, you will never achieve your dreams. And if you only ever listen to hope and never to reality, you will live in a dream world. It is by bringing the two together and allowing hope to have a little bit more of your time that you'll find the life you're searching for.

It is not wrong to be a dreamer, but it can be bad for us to be continually living in our dreams and never in reality. Our dreams will only be achieved with action in the real world with hope by our side. Live in reality, but live with hope and dreams in your heart and all that you hope to discover you will find. It is only a matter of time.

… 50

ELECTRICITY

We are not just a body; we are a body of energy. And if everything is energy, then we are all the same.

We hold electricity in our bodies and our minds. This electricity is energy we can use if we can see it in this way. Some may see this electricity as just energy. Untouchable, unusable, and beyond our reach, which is not the case. The electricity within us is just an extension of ourselves to all other elements and creatures in the universe.

We are not who we think we are. We are not just a body; we are a body of energy. And if everything is energy, then we are all the same. We are all beings of light and energy, and where one creature ends, another begins. If you can see and understand that we are all energy, then the limitations we place on ourselves no longer exist.

When we begin as a being of light, we choose how we will energetically manifest ourselves here on Earth. While one being may manifest as a lake, another might manifest as a human. The manifestation is what we appear as, but underneath we are all the same: energy and electricity. If we can learn to see ourselves as energy and not as dense objects, we can change many things, including illnesses, how we interact with the Earth and what is possible for us.

While we may need a physical body here on Earth, we must learn to ignore this to a point because if our attention is always taken by the material, we can never fully see the energetic. If you think of smoke, smoke can be thick or thin, layered, or swirling, fast or slow. Just as smoke looks different to each human eye, so do all creatures here on Earth. And just as smoke can change itself in a second, so can you. This is the nature of being a body of energy.

If we are sick, we can transmute and transform sickness into wellness. If we are depressed, we can transmute and transform depression into wellness and happiness. Part of life here is learning how to use your energy and electricity to interact and change with your environment.

Experiment with seeing your body as a body of energy. To begin, start viewing your body in this way, using your mind to make changes and move the energy like you would move smoke with your hand. Experiment with this, and then you can begin to learn more.

51

FEAR AND EGO

Remember that above all else, you are spirit and it is the ego that fights to give you a name, a title, a place in this world.

The fears you have do not define you, nor should they. You are not your fears, and your fears are not you. Your fears are your ego acting in disguise.

The ego's job on Earth for each human is to help propel them forward. You do not find the path to enlightenment, however with the ego. The ego's job is to get you as far as it can, but then it is your job to branch off on your own. The ego does not know this though as it believes it is the one in control and you are its servant. As human beings, more often than not, we do what the ego wants, but this comes at a price, just as all things come at a price.

When the ego makes decisions for us, our spirit has no part in that decision. When the ego dreams of money, power, and living the good life, our spirit wants to strip everything back, opting for simplicity over choice. When we go through the awakening process, part of this process is the spirit's needs becoming as prominent as the ego's needs. What the ego wants, spirit says we do not need, which creates conflict, and it is you who must decide who wins. Do you opt into the ego's wishes, knowing that it consumes only what it wants and will keep driving you to consume as long as you live? Or do you choose spirit, fight the ego daily, and seek out the simplicity that spirit offers?

The ego will never go away, as it lives inside you, but it can become quieter. From a toddler throwing a tantrum to a sleeping baby, the ego can be tamed into submission, but only if the spirit is strong and empowered enough to help you make that choice. Earth is a place full of ego, but that is what you are here to learn. You are here to learn that while ego serves its purpose for a time in propelling you forward, there comes the point where ego hinders your growth, and you must put it aside.

Before we come to Earth, we are spirit. When we

arrive on Earth, we forget spirit and become ego. Your objective on Earth is to remember you are more than ego; you are spirit. If you succeed in becoming spirit, the veil on Earth will be lifted, and you will see what life is like beyond living in a world where ego rules. Here you will see that you can be untouched by a humanity driven by ego. You will notice the simplicity of life. You will see that you can be happy, but in truth, there is no happiness, you just are.

If you are in a battle with the ego, stay strong. It is a daily battle, but it is worthwhile. Remember that above all else, you are spirit, and it is the ego that fights to give you a name, a title, a place in this world. While these things are needed, when you mature, you will understand you do not need them, and your spirit is unique enough on its own.

Eventually, the battle will become a fight, a fight an argument, and an argument a discussion. And finally there will be quiet, perhaps even peace, but there is no peace without struggle. Otherwise, we would not know what peace is when we find it.

Remember that each thought and the voice in your head is your ego, not your spirit. The spirit does not speak; it just is, as it is the purest version of you. It is the version that does need or want for anything.

If you can realize the voice and your desires are your ego, then you can decide if the ego is correct in its desires or not. Like the toddler needs discipline, so does your ego. Like the toddler needs to know when it is time for bed, so does the ego.

Recognize there are two presences inside you and always choose the presence that seeks only good for you, and that is spirit. The ego accumulates, the spirit sheds. If you can recognize this, you will find your way.

52

MOVEMENT

In time you will realise how much time you give to things that do not need your attention.

Movement indicates that there is growth in some way, but this is not always the case as there is movement and perceived movement, just as there is growth and perceived growth. The difference is whether we are moving and also changing in our minds and our hearts.

We can move at a hurried pace, but still feel like we are getting nowhere. Or, we can move and on closer assessment, get nowhere, and this can spark change.

If we look at our movement, analytically, critically, it doesn't take much to see that we spend our lives running in circles. Yet if we were to look at the circles we run in, we would see patterns emerge.

Each circle indicates something we need to learn, and we will continue to move in that circle until change occurs. However, if you can elevate yourself above the circle, even for a brief moment, you will see the nature of the ring you are running in. It is when we realize the nature of what we are doing and the 'mistakes' we are making, we can begin to change them. But if we cannot even see the mistakes, how can we be expected to improve?

Because of the nature of the universe and the limitlessness of our spirit, we can be running in many different circles at the same time. See each circle from above, identify the mistakes you are making, and this will eventually lead to the life lesson you are trying to overcome. You do not need to break each circle to move to the next one. All you need to do is recognize each circle for what it is and then begin making changes accordingly.

In time you will realize how much energy you give to things that do not need your attention. This comes from a lack of self-love and trying to satisfy an ego that will never be satisfied. The more circles the ego has you running in, the less chance you have of making a change, and the ego knows this, so remember it. The ego's job is to keep you busy, so you never see your spirit.

Know that you are spirit. Know the tricks the ego uses to keep you playing like a kitten with a ball of wool. Once you can see this and continue to notice it daily, you will create movement, change and progress.

53

FRIENDSHIP

Friendships are not limited to human beings. Those who can see the world for what it truly is, alive, can have a friendship with the Earth.

We may have friendships with all who exist in the world, whether they be human beings, plants, animals, or spirits. Friendship is available to those who seek it in all forms. To find friendship, we must first extend our hand and ask.

If we can develop a friendship with all of those around us, including the environment in which we live, our lives will be much healthier and more satisfying. If we see ourselves as alive and, therefore, only develop friendships with those we also see to be alive, we are missing out on incredible friendships with other elements in our environment that are also living.

Would you like to learn the wisdom of plant spirits? Would you like to listen to the water tell you stories of the sea? Would you enjoy hearing a one-thousand-year-old tree or rock tell you what it has seen in its time on Earth?

Friendships are not limited to human beings. Those who can see the world for what it truly is, alive, can have a friendship with the Earth. Those who wish to serve the Earth must have friends in all places and must seek to help those in all places.

You need not be able to hear the whisperings of a tree or plant to have a friendship with these creatures. Instead, extend your hand and let them know you are there if they need you. Let them know that you see them for what they truly are and that you wish to learn from them. If the day is hot, give them water. If the day is cold, send them love. Trees, plants, and other creatures are no different to humans in the sense that they also need companionship, love, and kindness.

Treat everything as your friend, and you will have no shortage of friendships. Life is both too short and too long not to see the fantastic creations all around you.

Take this knowledge and begin anew. Be a protector to not only human beings, but plants, trees, insects, animals, and all other living creatures too. When you need help, they will do the same for you.

54

TRANSIENT BEINGS

Transient beings are not tied to any one place or plane in particular and will continue to bring new knowledge hoping to eventually break through, just as they have done for many thousands of years before.

When you are a transient being, you move between states and places.

Transient beings are all around us in our world. They come to Earth and to our spiritual plane to learn and then continue to move on, much like the Wanderers do. Transient beings bring new knowledge with them from other planes, but whether we accept this knowledge is up to us.

On Earth, we accept all beings into our space. Even

those that do not have a good reputation in the universe. We believe Earth is a place of redemption for all spirits. When we encounter transient beings, we will not know as even they do not know themselves. They merely hold information that has come from before their birth.

Other beings on Earth who are interested in money and power aim to close off new ideas as ways of earning money have already been established on Earth, and they do not wish for other beings to complicate this. I am referring to such things as free energy. Free energy is something that should be available to all on Earth, especially given that we are all energetic beings. However, some humans see this as a threat, and have worked to remove new information and technology many times. This, unfortunately, is the way of Earth.

We are all here to learn lessons from each other and our experience here. Transient beings are not tied to any one place or plane in particular and will continue to bring new knowledge, hoping to eventually breakthrough, just as they have done for many thousands of years before.

When you see new technology or ideas that do not seem to be from this plane, they are likely not.

Accept these ideas, state your interest in them, and try to help ensure they see the light of day. One day the technology and concepts destined for Earth will make their way back here as the traditional structures and ways of life we rely on will eventually fall.

Look for transient beings and try to understand their ideas. The more people who openly share these ideas will eventually pave the way for these ideas and technologies to come to life.

55

LIFESTYLE

Life begins when we can see and understand that life is not defined by what we own, but by who we are when we are stripped back to our core.

When you have a lifestyle, you have a chosen state of living. When you have a lifestyle, you can become trapped in that chosen state of living. What starts off as pleasure can soon turn into pain. We make promises to people of the type of lifestyle we will live, and what this creates is a measure of whether we are living well or living poorly. Truthfully, there is no such thing as living well or living poorly as we are all merely living.

The trappings of committing to a particular lifestyle can mean you no longer have the sense of freedom you once had. If you can free yourself from these ideas and know that how you live doesn't matter, then you can take your first steps away from this regime of living. If you can re-establish who you are beyond what you currently live for, then you are better able to establish the boundaries of what you will and won't do to live.

When you can take a stand for your future self of what you do and do not want moving forward, then a line can be drawn in the sand, which you can step over when you are ready.

The lifestyle we believe we must keep up is an illusion and one that our ego creates for us. If we can understand this, just as a ball of wool is made, it can also be unrolled and undone. Start with the basic things. Discard all that you do not need and release it with gratitude. Discard everything connected to the part of you that wants to keep up with society. When you start releasing all you do not need, you will begin to see what matters in your life. You will start to see life outside of the construct you have created in your mind and your world. Life will begin to fill up with wonder again, and you will feel freer.

There is only a certain amount of time that one can continue to keep up with society, and this is a losing game. It is addictive, and the more you want, the more you can't have as your resources will always be limited. If, however, you can realize that real joy lies within, life will transform like never before. You will stop focussing on what is around you and start concentrating on what lies within. This is freedom: the freedom to choose, to begin again, to love yourself and others.

Life will be renewed if you choose to renew your life. All of life is energy, and when you start moving that energy around, you will naturally begin to see changes. If we only change what is on the surface, life will remain the same. If we can release all that is on the surface and show our true selves, life begins to change from within, which is what we wish for you.

To transform your life, you must shed all that you do not need. By doing this, you are clearing anything that may stop the path to enlightenment appearing before you. Life begins when we can see and understand that life is not defined by what we own, but by who we are when stripped back to our core. This is spirit. Spirit does not want for material things. Spirit knows that material things do not lead to joy; they lead to addiction and a constant need for 'more.'

You may not have met spirit yet, but know that it exists and wishes to meet you as you are, not the lifestyle you have become accustomed to.

HARMONY

To find who we are and to be in harmony, we must accept that harmony encompasses happiness as much as hell.

When you are in harmony, you are at one with the universe. There is no separation between you and the world around you. Both melt together like two liquids becoming one.

What separates us from being in harmony is the view we have of ourselves and humanity. When we believe we are unique or different from others, we separate ourselves from them. When we see ourselves through the lens of the ego, we see the picture our ego has created for us, which is not real. It is a painting that changes continuously, as per the ego's wishes.

The ego wishes for us to be happy enough to have a taste of happiness and sad enough always to be craving more, which creates a whirlwind of emotion and one we are always trying to calm or undo. We are taught to dream of finding a place where only sunshine exists and storms never pass, but this place does not exist. Even the most enlightened souls on Earth still experience pain and suffering.

To find who we are and to be in harmony, we must accept that harmony encompasses happiness as much as hell. Harmony is both. However, when we see ourselves as part of everything else, we can become an energy that moves with both, not pushes against it. It is when we move against pain and suffering that we experience more of this. It is when we fight these emotions of the human condition that we create a tornado, living in the eye of the storm with chaos all around us.

The sun that happiness brings is always on the horizon but never feels obtainable because it is not. Seeing it on the horizon does not mean we cannot experience it and bring happiness into our hearts. Just as we happily and joyfully experience a beautiful sunrise and sunset and let the colors fill us up.

When we fight against pain and suffering, we only

see pain and suffering as this is the chaos we create in our own lives by fighting forces bigger and stronger than us. If we can accept that pain and suffering will exist, no matter how enlightened we become, there is no tornado. If we can embrace pain and suffering, wholeheartedly and accept that we are the same as everything else on Earth, we will not see pain; we will only see the changing of colors.

What this does is dissipate the tornado, leaving a grey sky that will eventually turn back to the pinks and oranges we have come to know and love.

Do not fight pain or suffering as you will never win. When you fight pain and suffering, the tornado grows in strength and power, which in turn fuels the ego, none of which we want. If you give yourself over to both pain and happiness, the tornado cannot gather in strength, as there are no opposing forces, just a simple change in the color of the sky. One we know will pass as we can never stay at sunset, just as we can never remain in the rain. All seasons and all weathers will pass.

If you experience a season of winter, know this will pass. If you experience a season of summer, know this will pass too. Also, remember that spring and autumn exist, and you will experience these as well.

What we experience with our emotions is very similar to what we experience with the seasons, and even those who are enlightened still experience the coldest of winters and hottest of summers. Know there is beauty in both, as both are different and bring alternative challenges and moments to learn from.

57

MAGIC

When we can see ourselves as spirit, life is forever changed.

Magic is what you feel within and out. It is your spirit and how you display your spirit to the world. When we feel the magic within us, everything is possible, and nothing is impossible. Believing in our magic ensures we live a positive and meaningful life.

When we lack in magic, it means we lack belief in our spirit. It means that we do not see the spirit; we see the body. The body is merely an energetic representation of who and what we are here on Earth, but it is not us in the most real sense. The body is limited by what it can do with its arms, legs, hands, and head, whereas the spirit is unlimited, just as life is unlimited.

When we can see ourselves as spirit, life is forever changed. We no longer look at what we can do with our arms, legs, hands, and head, we look at what we can do with our heart and our soul and the impact we can make.

If you wish to find the magic inside you, you must believe you are more than a body and a presence here on Earth. You must believe you are a spirit, and the spirit is unlimited. Where the body remains primarily the same, the spirit can change and morph into all manner of things.

The spirit is not defined by its beliefs, or its abilities to do or not do, succeed or not succeed. The spirit simply is. When you see yourself as energy, you can transform and transmute all parts of yourself. Nothing is off-limits. You are no longer confined to ideas of the body; you are free to explore the ideas of the universe.

Just because you live here on Earth, does not mean that you cannot be a universal spirit full of magic. Just because you live on Earth, do not believe that you cannot accomplish all that you dream of. All is possible if you believe there is magic within and the magic begins the moment you see yourself as spirit. The magic becomes a force for good in your life and the lives of others when you no longer look at your body as a limitation, but as a gateway to all that could be possible.

Life presents us with many options, and how you see yourself is one of those options. If you continue to look at yourself as a body, you will live as a body. If you see yourself as a spirit, you can move around all that you previously saw and create something new, magical, and untamed. This is what we wish for you, the transformation from body to body of energy.

Take this new knowledge and play with it. Begin thinking about what is possible if you are energy and not a body. You will be surprised by what is possible.

LUCK

To create luck, luck needs a destination for you to aspire to reach.

Luck is not just for those who find it. It is everywhere, in the trees, the sunlight, the moon, and the stars. Luck is not born; it is made. It is made in the creation of desires and the synchronicity of when a human being, plant, or animal wishes for change and moves with their environment to create it.

When you put energy into the universe, it is like planting seeds that will eventually bear fruits. It is throwing a pebble into a river, knowing that eventually it will be carried to a new shore. We do not stumble across luck; we make it. If you wish to create more luck or synchronicity in your life, then you must create it, but first, you must decide what you wish for and what you wish to achieve or find. To create luck, luck needs a destination you're aspiring to reach.

If you know or have an idea of what your destination is, then you begin dreaming and plan how you will get there. Each thought or idea you have is a seed to be planted or a pebble to be thrown. As you plant each seed and throw each pebble, you will begin to notice more seeds and pebbles. When the earth covers the seed, and the river takes the pebble downstream, for a while, it will seem like nothing is happening. But then, out of nowhere, you will catch a glimpse of what is coming.

At this point, rather than stopping, you should continue to throw more seeds and pebbles, as you have created the momentum you need to produce luck and synchronicity. When you give to the universe, the universe gives back, which is what all human beings need to know and remember. Love creates luck, and luck creates love. Both are cyclical and are free to all human beings to access. If we do not believe in luck, we do not believe in love. However, what we must all remember and understand is that luck is made by us, through lovingly caring for the dreams and wishes we do have. If you can take what I have taught you about luck, then use this knowledge now to begin creating luck in your own life.

Luck and life are what you make it. Nothing happens by chance, and nothing will ever happen by chance. Choose to create luck, and you will create a happy life. Life is not made by sitting back and waiting for it to come to you; you must create your life.

You can drink from the cup of life, but only if you replenish the water you have taken. Learn to create luck, and you will lead a happy life.

FREEDOM

It is only when we see imperfection in others that we can see the imperfection and perfection in ourselves.

Before you are born, you have the opportunity to decide who you will be born to. This is free will, and this is the freedom you are given in the sky and here on Earth.

Before you are born, there are many sets of parents you can be born to, but you choose them based on the life lessons you wish to learn in this life. It is a choice that is made easier by you in the sky because no matter how hard the challenges your parents will bring, in the sky you have the foresight to know how the story will end.

If you chose parents who would serve you well, you chose a life that would present challenges. If you chose parents who would not serve you well, you have also chosen a life with challenges. It is the role of parents and those around you to teach the life lessons you have asked to learn. What you have is the freedom to choose how you will learn these lessons, the attitude you will approach the lessons with, how fast or slowly you wish to learn, and how deeply you will ponder each lesson.

It is your parents that give you your will, but also your way. It is your parents who will challenge you with their love and hate for themselves and others. It is your parent's truths, strengths, mastery, and lack of mastery that will teach you what you wish to learn here.

It may not always be ideal, just as life is not ideal, but would you wish for it to be any other way? We need those who are imperfect for us to love ourselves in a perfect way. It is only when we see imperfection in others that we can see the imperfection and perfection in ourselves. We are all perfect, yet we are all imperfect, and this is what we want you to learn.

When you are young, you may put your parents on a pedestal, holding them high in your head and your heart. As time goes on, you discover that they are imperfect and are also learning as they go. It is through their mistakes that you will learn. It is through their mistakes with you that you will grow. This is because adversity is needed to learn here on Earth. It is fire that creates diamonds, and it is only after the storm do we appreciate brilliant sunlight.

There are many types of freedom; however, freedom from your parents comes at a cost to both of you. You both must learn to love yourselves unconditionally. Life is pure; life is perfect; life is free if you wish it to be.

When we can release ourselves and our parents from past hurt, pain, we too can be free, and this is when we will have learned our lesson. Parents are our teachers, but they are also our students. When you can see that the parent is not the protector, they are the teacher; then, we may be free. When we as parents can learn from our children, then we can also be free. Free to love, to learn, and free to learn to love ourselves.

Life is pure and free, but only when we wish it and work it to be. Enjoy life, enjoy love, enjoy the lessons your parents teach you, just as you teach them.

60

GAINS AND LOSSES

Know that where you find losses, you will find gains. Know that when losses appear, gains are never far away.

When we experience gains and losses, we win, and then we lose. We make progress, and then we fail. This is the way of life, just as it is the way of love. When we win, we learn how it feels to win. We feel the sensation of empowerment, choice, and freedom. Freedom to stop or freedom to go again. Most of all, when we win, we experience love for ourselves and others.

When we lose, we experience loss in every sense of the word. We feel pain, pain at what we could have achieved and gained, and grief at what we have lost. When we lose, it is like winning and losing at the same time. If we can learn to see gains and losses everywhere, we can learn to accept that our life will contain a balance of gains and losses, even when the amount does not seem balanced.

Human beings break people into winners and losers. Some appear to win at everything and some seem to lose. In the sky, we do not define who will be a winner and who will be a loser, because these terms do not exist to us. It is a human construct and a human idea. What we define is experiences and experiences either make or break people. There are those who create their own luck and those who sit and wait for the tsunami to hit. This is not right or wrong; it is simply the journey they have chosen in this life.

If we can choose to create our luck, no matter what the circumstances are or the pain we are in, we can become luckier and win more. This is the way the universe works when you contribute to it.

There are those in environments where there is war, pain, famine, and death, yet they somehow manage to find light in themselves and those around them. They are not unique and have not been given gifts that make their minds think this way; they have created light for themselves and others. They have accepted that life is pain, and pain is life. When you can learn to see life in this way, you will learn to expect pain and suffering, but you will also expect to see the sun and its beautiful sunrises and sunsets.

There are gains, and there are losses. In your life here on Earth, you will experience both. Know they are even in their amount even if you do not see them, and they are here to teach you and push you to learn. To learn is what we wish for you.

If you do not learn, there is no point coming to Earth. Earth is a place for learners, for teachers, and we experience the gains and losses we need to fulfill our time and our master plan here on Earth.

Know that where you find losses, you will see gains. Know that when losses appear, gains are never far away. If you continue to plant seeds of hope and abundance, you can choose to see the light in all situations.

61

CHERISH

When we let ourselves sink deep into all that we are and all that we can be, we attract teachers worth cherishing.

We ask that you cherish your teachers, just as you cherish your students.

There are those that will lead you and those that you will lead into the sun. There are those who will give their time and believe in you at no cost to you. Just as you believe in them, you will cherish each other for what this relationship brings.

When we cherish, we pay respect to what has been taught and what can be taught. When we cherish, we experience gratitude at the teachings available to us. We must cherish our teachers and the gifts they give us.

To cherish is to give your love, kindness, and respect to another. To give your pain to another to carry for a time or a moment. To cherish is to trust, to accept and be grateful for the gifts you have received and the gifts you will receive. If we can find those worthy of cherishing, we are lucky as they are hard to find but easy to keep if you cherish them. If you ask to find someone worth cherishing, they will find you, but only if you show gratitude and respect.

When we let ourselves sink deep into all that we are and all that we can be, we attract teachers worth cherishing. If we can accept that who we think we can be goes even deeper than we ever imagined, then only a teacher who has gone deeper can show you how deep and limitless you are as a mind, body, and spirit.

We must look for teachers, however, who can show us our spirit and those who can reveal it to us in ways we can understand. If you have not found a teacher who can show you your spirit, then ask, and the teacher will appear. If you ask, you will receive. This is the way.

In time, we will learn, just as we cherished our teachers at school, that we may also find teachers in our adult life to cherish. We are all learners, and we are here on Earth to learn. If you wish to find the path to enlightenment, you must find great teachers and guides who can show you the way as each has their own experience of life here on Earth.

The path can be lit, but only by those who have been there before. We can, of course, learn a lot on our own, but we can learn more from a teacher who challenges and supports us than we can teach ourselves. Thousands of teachers around the world have already lit the path. Find one which suits you but also challenges you. We can only learn from those who make us learn and from those who have the power to turn our glance inwards, not outwards.

Life and the path to enlightenment are to be discovered, but you must be willing to learn to find it. Life is a question and an answer all in a single breath. The path can be as long as it can be windy, so it is best to have a companion on the journey now and in the future, as you too may be the teacher if you are willing to learn.

62

MISFORTUNE

If we expect our lives to be fortunate, we must understand that fortune is made up of misfortune.

When we experience misfortune, we believe that the universe is working against us. It is not; it is merely asking us to look deeper within. Misfortune is life's way of making us pay attention because sometimes we wander mindlessly, only ever looking at our feet and not at the sky.

In our life, we will experience misfortune. This is guaranteed as fortunate or misfortunate this may seem. Misfortune is designed to make us humble, to help us understand that life or its circumstances are not permanent. Life is as fleeting and changing as the clouds are in the sky. Life can be molded, but then the mold can also break.

If we expect our lives to be fortunate, we must understand that fortune is made up of misfortune. If we experience misfortune, we must also recognize that to experience misfortune; we must have also found fortune. Life is both light and darkness, fortune, and misfortune. There are places in the middle where life is neither fortune or misfortune. It is this place in the middle that is called life.

If you experience misfortune, accept it gratefully with both hands and an open heart. If you experience fortune, also receive it with both hands and an open heart. When you are stuck in the middle in the place that feels neither here or there, accept this too with an open heart as you can learn as much about yourself in the middle as you can on either side.

On Earth, we try to give you a backbone of experiences, and as you will know, the backbone of life contains both joy and pain. We will provide you with the spectrum as that is what we promised you in your time here. Neither is a gift or a punishment. It just is.

63

FEARS

Through our fears we come to know ourselves and understand our true potential.

When we are on the path to enlightenment, it is natural that we will experience fear.

It is natural to experience fear because we are treading a path we have not traveled. We do not know who or what is around the next corner. We also do not know when we will meet our true self.

Meeting our true self is something we all fear. Most would believe it's exciting to meet who we truly are, however, this is not necessarily the case because the person we meet is not always the person we expect. When I say this, I am not speaking of deep dark secrets, I speak of our fear of the profound potential that lies within us.

What we tend to fear most is not the self we wake up with every day, but the self not driven by what other people want, need or hope to see from us. It is the self that is free from all judgment, pain, and suffering. The self who wishes for love and a life of love. The self who does not see limitations, but sees obstacles as gifts and the self that is wise, kind and true.

During our life and lives on Earth, we spend most of our time creating masks. Masks hide who we truly are when the journey of being on Earth is to discover who we are not. Only when we put down our masks can we discover who we are. Finding out who you are not is a painful process. We experience pain because of the time we invest in believing our own stories of who we think we should be. When our body, mind, and soul recognize who we are not, this is painful because there is a moment when we do not know who we are at all. There is no context and nothing to reach for or hold. At this moment, we are more ourselves than ever because we are without identity. Who we think we are is an idea or concept of ourselves created by the ego.

In the moments when we do not know who we are, we are closer to spirit than ever. If we can breathe during this time, it can be enjoyable, but for most people, this can be one of the most uncomfortable and fearful times of their lives.

Not knowing who you are is not easy. Knowing who you think you are is not easy either. The place in the middle is when we find rest. If we can be comfortable knowing who we are is never who we think, life will become easier. If we can be comfortable in the pain of ambiguity and live in this space, life will be kinder to us. The more we cling to an idea, the more this idea works to prove itself untrue. The more we can accept we are constantly in flux, the more we can begin to accept we do not need to know who we are, we just are.

Fear is something people avoid on Earth because this one emotion wraps up all that we know and do not know about our past, present and our future. In our fears, we lose ourselves, and in our fears we find ourselves.

On Earth, we are taught to look for the positive and to ignore the negative parts of ourselves. If we can learn to look at the negative objectively, we can discover the deeper parts of ourselves that have not yet surfaced. If you are looking for answers, here is where you will find them. Through our fears, we come to know ourselves and understand our true potential. If we can have the courage not to look away or flinch, life can be very different from the life we know now.

Embrace your fears, love your weaknesses and look deeply into what you fear the most. Look beneath the masks you create. Through the masks you create you will know what you have been subconsciously trying to hide. It is under these masks that you will find your most significant challenges and successes. If you face your fears, you will be proud of yourself. If you do not face your fears, you will run from them forever, and no amount of masks will stop that chase.

Learn to love your fears as they will teach you more about yourself than anyone on this Earth can. Hide, and your fears will come looking for you anyway. Stand in your fear, in your pain and sorrow, and you will find light. Love always finds light.

64

INTERRUPTIONS

The wisest way to travel is to plan for interruptions, challenges, bad weather and for getting lost along the way.

Your life and your path will continuously be interrupted, but is this not life?

The spiritual path is not a linear one. It is winding, and the weather can sometimes be extreme. What we must look for in troubled or challenging times is our destination or the destination we have in mind for that day. This is what we ask you to focus on.

Where do you wish to travel today, beyond the interruptions that will no doubt slow down your journey?

The wisest way to travel is to plan for interruptions, challenges, bad weather and for getting lost along the way. This journey is not a perfect one, nor should it be. What you are being tested on is your ability to stay focused no matter what life throws at you.

The skills you've been given are a gift, but they do not make you immune to life's more annoying and interruptive aspects. Do not be hard on yourself for getting frustrated or angry. Instead, challenge yourself to keep moving forward despite life's interruptions. This is the ultimate test.

In time you will come to learn that every experience, big and small makes up the entire journey. Each experience works to build the whole. Therefore, do not look at interruptions as interruptions, look at them as necessary parts of your life and what makes you human.

65

YOUR UNSPEAKABLE TRUTH

To speak your unspeakable truth is brave in a world that contains so much fear.

When you are speaking your unspeakable truth, you are revealing your true self and voice. When you speak your unspeakable truth, you help others to speak theirs. When you allow yourself to be who you are, you allow others to be themselves too.

Life and other people do not make it easy on those who speak their truth. This is, unfortunately, the way on Earth. Earth is a place of much beauty, but we are often asked not to speak as what we say can make others uncomfortable. Life is uncomfortable. Not speaking your truth is uncomfortable. If we never spoke our truth, the world would never change, people would never allow themselves to be who they were born to be.

To speak your unspeakable truth is to say what is on your mind and in your heart that is unspoken. It is to speak your mind and your heart with kindness and love, knowing that your words may be met with deaf ears. To speak your unspeakable truth is brave in a world that contains so much fear. To speak when you are not asked to is to gift the world with your song. A bird does not ask before it sings, it merely sings and it is a truthful song.

As human beings, we hide our emotions constantly. This damages us and the world. The Earth needs people who will speak for those who cannot speak for themselves.

If you wish to begin your journey to enlightenment, you must learn to listen and to speak. Not the words the world wants to hear, but your own words, experience, and truth. Truth is not truth if it is molded for what the listener is willing to hear. Truth is only truth if it is spoken honestly, openly and with love. Truth is only truth if it is pure and unfiltered, delivered with warm hands and a kind heart.

Learning to speak your truth is one of the most important gifts and skills you will develop in your life. Dedicate time to it and life will give you much in return.

66

COURAGE

Your life can have as much or as little impact as you wish it to have. It is only limited by how courageous you are.

If you wish to undertake the path to enlightenment, you will need courage. Courage in your convictions, courage that your direction is right and the courage to get up again when you are pushed down.

As we have spoken about before, this path is not for the faint of heart, nor should it be. The path to enlightenment welcomes those who are courageous of heart, but also those who are not courageous yet. Courage takes time to grow. What we look for is a purity of spirit and heart. It is those who contain this purity who we will take under our wing and help to grow to be more courageous than they ever imagined they could be.

When we are courageous, we can undertake quests we never thought possible. This is a quest. When you think of yourself, you already know you have courage, yet you wouldn't see yourself as courageous. This is the next leap, from acts of courage to being courageous.

When we have courage, we believe in ourselves and we are strong enough to have a voice. Not a voice that is projected loudly on a stage, but a voice within that is prepared to stand up and be heard, whether it be through action, writing or song. When we are courageous, we are prepared to take on the world. Not in the way of you versus the world, but in a way that nothing the world could say would scare you from your path or from having your voice heard.

If you can learn to transform acts of courage into living courageously, the sky is the limit of what you could accomplish. Human beings are so limited by fear that seventy percent of what we dream of is achievable, yet we never try because of what we think of ourselves or what we believe others will think of us. What if you could accomplish that extra seventy percent? What would you do with your life, with the world, with the world's people, animals, and plants?

You can continue to have courage and you would achieve a lot. However, we ask that you begin practicing what it is like to live courageously.

A good way to be more courageous is to do the opposite of what you would do on most days. What if you put fear aside and did what you wanted to? What if you stopped thinking about what other people would think and instead thought about what you would think of yourself if you did all you dreamed of? What would your loved ones think if you become an unstoppable force for change in this world, not defined by a filter of what is or isn't appropriate?

Your life can have as much or as little impact as you wish it to have. It is only limited by how courageous you are.

How courageous do you wish you could be? This is your answer and this place is possible for you to reach. Start by introducing small acts of courage every day. This is how you begin. Slowly but surely courage will transform into being courageous.

To live a full life we must be brave, to live a life of impact, we must be courageous.

67

MADNESS

When we all become involved in the drama, there is no-one left to undo it.

The world is in a state of madness, and you can choose to take part in this or step back thoughtfully.

When we participate in the madness, we become part of it. When we take a step back thoughtfully, we become observers from afar, better able to make decisions and act wisely.

The Earth has and always will be in various states of madness and this is the illusion. However, you have the power to choose to or not to take part. The wisest of you will step back and ask how you can help, but not drown in it. Those who are not wise enough to step back will become consumed by it. The symptoms of being consumed by madness are constant anxiety, pain, and fear. Those who can step back, purposefully and thoughtfully will begin to notice that the further you step back, the more peaceful you become. The more peaceful you become, the more you can act out of a place of love, offering to help not hinder humanity's efforts.

When we all become involved in the drama, there is no-one left to undo it. This is what we wish for you to do. See the madness as a spinning ball of wool that needs to be unwound. To unwind it, you cannot be inside the ball of wool. You must be outside of it and be able to pull the string to see the ball unravel.

Remember that you are most potent when you step outside of the circumstances you see and you are most weak when you are stuck inside.

We have the power, and we are empowered to choose what we become involved in and what we do not. This is your choice, and it always has been. Do not believe those who say that you do not have a choice as they are already inside the ball of wool. Those who are inside will invite more in and those who are outside are able to invite those that are stuck back out.

If you wish to help the Earth and yourself, you will

stay out of the madness and look at it from afar. See how you can best help, first from the position of the observer, then from a place of action. The key is to always act from the position of pulling the string and not trying to break the ball down from the inside. This never has and will never work. Be inspired by those already acting from outside of the ball of wool. See what they do and take guidance from them. Learn to see and recognize those who are stuck inside. They do not know any better, but there is a way out for them if they choose it.

The world is in a state of madness, but we do not need to choose to be part of it. We can instead be part of the solution, but solutions must be created from the outside to work their way in.

68

BEING OPEN

In your life, you will have experiences that both build and break you. Our job is to give you the support you need to carry on.

When we are born with spiritual gifts, we should not expect them to come as planned. Often we have an idea in our mind of what we want or desire our spiritual gifts to be, yet it is often the most unplanned and unexpected gifts that bring us the most joy.

When we accept these gifts in our body and our mind, we should receive them with grace, humility and quiet confidence. We would not be given these gifts if we were not ready for them, nor should we ever feel undeserving.

We see every act you do on this Earth. We hear every

word you speak, every thought you manifest and every idea you have. We feel and see your intentions, your heartbreaks, triumphs and your perceived failures. In your life, you will have experiences that both build and break you. Our job is to give you the support you need to carry on.

You did not come to this Earth to relax and have a good time. While we want you to do both of these, the purpose of you coming to Earth is to learn about yourself and the world around you. In times of change, look to past experiences of triumph and to us to know you will get through. Sometimes scathed or unscathed, sometimes with significant or little spurts of growth.

We are proud of you no matter what you achieve. In the context of all of your lives, you have accomplished much. Whether you see this in this life or the next, you are already great in our eyes. What we wish for is that you experience love, humility and grace. What we wish for you to offer others is the same. What we wish for you to provide yourself with is the same. We tend to disregard our own needs and cater more to the needs of others than we do ourselves. Know that while we want you to take care of others, we want you to take care of yourself too. This is important.

Be open to pain, to progress and to always knowing there is more to life than what you can see. The package you are as a human being now is always changing, therefore do not be tied to who you are now as who you are now will not be who you are tomorrow.

Life presents us with many changes and challenges. Accept both, love both and know that with each step forward you are becoming more of who you were always destined to be.

69

MASKS

You are unique. In all of your lives there has only been one of you.

When we wear masks, we are hiding. Sometimes from others, sometimes from the person we fear we may be. As human beings, we are born with DNA which makes us unlike any other human being on Earth, yet we try to be like others. If we could embrace our uniqueness and what makes us irreplaceable, we would also embrace our true path on Earth.

The path we wish for you to seek is one of enlightenment and becoming more awake. The more you try to be like or compare yourself to someone else, the more asleep you fall. The less you enable your true self to come forward, the more unfinished business you will acquire. If you can accept that you are unique, you will stop looking to others to find out who you are. If you can accept this, you will no longer go in search of modeling yourself on someone else or the masters who have come before you.

You are unique. In all of your lives, there has only been one of you. This is the way.

For you to embrace who you are, you must first understand all that you are not. You are not anyone else on this Earth, nor do we wish for you to be. You are not me; you are not Buddha, you are not Jesus, you are not Allah. You are you, and there is no-one like you.

You have your distinct path, your way of looking at the world and your way of seeing is different from others' ways of seeing. What you hear is different from what others will hear. You are here to share your experience so that others may share theirs. If you accept that you are and cannot be like anybody else, you will stop trying to be someone else. You will stop measuring yourself against someone else, because what is there to measure when there is no metric or comparison. It is like trying to compare an apple with an orange. They are both fruit, but they are not the same.

To be happier, you must be happier with yourself. To feel loved, you must learn to love yourself, for all of your strengths, weaknesses, flaws, and failures. There is no other like you, and we are glad you were born this way. You all have an individual part to play on this Earth, and you can only play that part if you are you. Any imitation will not do. The more you compare yourself to others, the slower your journey will be. The more you wonder how you will measure up to others and what they will think of you when you are your true self, the slower your journey will be.

Embrace change and embrace it quickly. Embrace your true self and know that DNA makes you unique for a purpose and you will travel fast and well.

Love yourself. Cherish your differences. Make your mark on an Earth that desperately needs the gifts of those who were born to give. We love every one of you, and we ask you to step forward and play your part. Drop your masks, reveal your true self and your potential here is limitless.

70

ENTRY POINTS

We find ourselves not in the walking, but in the discoveries we make along the way, where there are no distractions, nothing trying to steal our attention and nothing to hide our pain and our joy.

There are many entry points onto the path to enlightenment. Most would think it has a beginning and an end, but you can enter at any part of the journey, and you will meet others along the way.

The path to enlightenment is one that can be steep, windy and on some days testing. Sometimes we walk onto the path and some days we walk off, depending on the experiences we are having in our everyday life. If we understand we have the ability to enter and exit at any time, it takes the pressure off finding the exact place the path begins. There is no exact place because the path to enlightenment is different for every human being. Unlike other pilgrimages and defined paths, there is no one set path.

We wish for you to create your journey, to follow your path. There is nothing we would like more than to see many people walking the path. However, this is every human being's choice, and some do not wish to walk the path in this lifetime. We cannot force those around us to walk with us, but we can invite them to do so.

When one enters the path, it is natural for some of the people around us to fall away and not understand our willingness to shed and find ourselves. Most would assume that to find happiness on Earth is to live a good, full life with lots of possessions. A life of accumulation. Life on the path to enlightenment is very different. On the path, we ask that you learn to shed all that you think you need and all that you think you are to learn all you are not.

The answer to your divine purpose here on Earth comes when you have nothing left to hide behind. It is only when we can see nothing else that we can see ourselves. Do not force those around you to join you. Simply invite them along the way. Walk on and off the path as you choose, as not all lessons are provided on the path. Some lessons need to be learned in the real world and not in the spiritual world. If you can learn this, the pressure will be removed.

Ideally, the path is one that you walk alone, bumping into old friends and new along the way. We cannot wish for more than your happiness and your fulfillment. Some will find this on the path; some won't. It is not up to us to choose who comes with us; we must make this choice for ourselves and only through choosing will we find what we are looking for.

We find ourselves not in the walking, but in the discoveries we make along the way, where there are no distractions, nothing trying to steal our attention and nothing to hide our pain and our joy. It is through finding ourselves that we will find our way back home.

ENERGY

If we do not feed the light, the light cannot grow.

The energy we carry projects itself onto the world like a beacon. If we project positive energy and abundance without fear of lack, we will attract more of the positive energy we project. It comes back to us.

If we project negative energy into the world, more negative energy will find us and will top up your cup with negative energy. It is this simple. If we can project more positive energy into the world, we are creating more positive energy that is circulated and returned to us. It is the reward for projecting more good into the world.

If we project negative energy, we become further entrenched in the negative energy that surrounds and drains us. It is for this reason that we must make a choice. Do we wish to project negative energy or positive energy, knowing that whatever we project comes back to us doubled or triple? It is important we make the right choices about what we project.

Understandably as human beings we can go through darker periods of our lives. Sometimes being cloaked in and projecting negative energy is all we can do as that is our reality. However, we can choose how long these feelings last by working through them, getting to the source of the issue and releasing it. This can be done through meditation, seeing a healer or by working through it in your mind. If you cannot work through it on your own, seek the help of another who can help you release it.

The longer you are cloaked in negative energy the harder it is to release it. The longer it surrounds you, the harder it is to peel it off you, which is where the role of shaman's and healers come in as they can work with both you and the sky to remove the energy and replace it with a clean slate. We cannot fill up the positive energy for you, but we can help you transmute the negative energy.

What we must remember in our day to day lives

is that what we send out comes back to us and depending on the lunar cycle its effects can amplify. Therefore, send out positive energy into the world, even if the last thing you feel like doing is being positive. This is an act of self-preservation as the light inside of you still needs feeding even when you do not feel like doing it.

Human beings have two sides: the light and the dark. Some days we may feel darker than others, but we must continue to feed and nurture the lighter parts of ourselves so we can grow in strength and come back into balance. If we do not feed the light, the light cannot grow. If we only ever feed the dark, we cannot expect anything less than the dark to take us over.

Accept that you have both light and dark within you, but choose to continue feeding the light no matter how you are feeling. The light is always a worthy companion on your journey.

72

PATHWAYS

Everything we need to heal ourselves lies within us, the Earth, and what manifests inside and around it. Find the healer, find the healing.

When you wish to find the path to enlightenment you must look for the pathways in. There are many ways to do this, but primarily it is opening your mind and heart to new possibilities in the healing space.

We are all natural healers, and by nature, we can heal ourselves if we have the right tools. When we give ourselves the right tools and techniques, we can revert to a time in our existence many lives ago when we did not see doctors; we saw healers.

Healers ensured our mind, body and soul health was at its best so that we could accomplish all we wished or needed to. This is the difference between healing of the past and medicine of the present and future. Doctors are a form of healer, but most are taught to heal what they can see in the body, not realizing that the issue may lie in the mind, emotions or the soul. When we work on the problems within, we solve what is manifesting in the physical body.

There are times and places for doctors, particularly with wound care and disease. However, if you feel that what you are dealing with could be an unresolved issue from your past, no matter how far back that is, you are best to find a healer to work with. There are many different types of healers.

You can see a shaman if you need pieces of your soul retrieved or if there are demons from your past that need to be met and extinguished. Shamans can also help with natural medicines and remedies. Shaman's work with the soul's past, present, and future to free the current version up to do the job it was destined to do.

You can see a plant healer if there are issues within the body that need resolving. A plant healer not only works with the medicine plants create but with the spirit of the plant which is a healer in its own rite.

If it is information you seek, then it is a messenger that you can help you retrieve the guidance you need to move forward.

There are many different types of healers around the world. What we must learn is not to look to a doctor in times of trouble automatically, but to the right healer. We are not saying that you do not need doctors. We are saying that a doctor is one form of healer, however, in our lives, we will need the help of many.

Meeting the right healer can resolve a lifelong issue. Seeing the wrong type of healer can result in a lifetime of dealing with a symptom, an illness or a life path blockage. Know that there are many different types of healers currently working all over the Earth. Seek them out, talk to them and if they are not the right healer for you right now, ask them who they would trust and recommend you see. This is the way.

Everything we need to heal ourselves lies within us, the Earth and what manifests inside and around it. Find the healer, find the healing.

LIGHT

If you wish to find more light in yourself, you must create more light in the world around you.

In our time here on Earth, we must choose to do light activities and not dark. When we do dark activities, we are creating more darkness which consumes the Earth. When we do light activities, we do well for the Earth because light feeds light.

Given that the Earth is a light planet at its core; light feeds the Earth. This is why we need more lightworkers on Earth to help shift the balance.

The Earth has been in disarray for a long time, leaving plants, animals and human beings in pain and high levels of suffering. People do not even know what true happiness is anymore as it is so fleeting in Earth's population. Even when we try and find it, we question if it is 'happiness'.

Happiness is a sense of peace, a sense of not needing or wanting for anything else. Happiness is a state of mind, not a moment as human beings think it is. Human beings dream of finding happiness, yet how can we hold onto it when it is so momentary. In time we will learn that happiness is not fleeting, it is a state of mind. One that is achievable with the right work and commitment.

If we do not invest hard work and dedication, we will naturally only experience fleeting moments of happiness and after we will go back into our oppression again.

If you wish to experience happiness for longer than a few seconds, question why it only exists for you for a few seconds. Question why it is so short and not so long that it goes on forever. Look to your environment, the people around you, the jobs that you keep, the lifestyle you have committed to. In each of these areas, there are triggers that end happiness as soon as it arrives. The more we can simplify our lives the more we can access happiness for longer.

The less we have to distract us, the more we can be at one with our environment and the people we love and who love us. The more we can let go of the 'shoulds' and 'coulds' in our life, the more likely we are just to be.

It is through being and being unattached to any outcome or avoiding pain that we can just be. To be in our environment, to be with our people and to be in our homeland.

If you wish to find more light in yourself, you must create more light in the world around you. It is through being and feeling lighter and creating more light that we can be free. Free to float and free to exist without any one person, thing or experience tying us down.

74

RIGIDITY

We should aim to be like fish in the river, moving up or downstream depending on where our journey takes us. When we become a rock in the river, we have become rigid.

When the mind becomes rigid, it becomes brittle. It no longer accepts new ideas, and the purpose of being on Earth is to accept new ideas and grow.

When we encounter those who are rigid, we must seek to expand and stretch their mind, even if this is uncomfortable for them to do so. It is important to recognize that there is a difference between pushing ideas onto someone, as this makes you rigid too, and stretching or pushing their comfort zone. We wish for you to push people's comfort zones as this is what helps Earth's community grow.

We know we have become rigid when we no longer accept new or outside ideas. We have become rigid when we no longer see ourselves as right or wrong, but like concrete, unchanging and unmoving. This is the state one ends up in when they have spent too much time moving against things and not with them.

We should aim to be like fish in the river, moving up or downstream depending on where our journey takes us. When we become a rock in the river, we have become rigid. When we can no longer move up or down the river, the sediment begins to gather around us, cementing us further into the ground.

There is a positive to holding our space, but not when stubbornness overcomes us, and we become a force that tries to stop the river from flowing. There are people all around you who are rocks in the river. There are also many people who are fish and those who only float with the current. To find your way you must find the fish. However, you must also not be afraid to travel on your own, as while the school brings you safety, safety is not where we push our boundaries and expand.

In time you will be able to see the entire river, not from within it, but from above and below. Here is where you will gain clarity. For now, however, find the fish, find strength in the school and then break away to find the unexplored parts of the river. Do not listen to the rocks and do not pay attention to the obstacles that may stand in your way.

Take time to grow, have fun and play. While life can become more serious, find time to relish in the opportunity to help others expand, just as they are helping you to expand. Take the time to meet others in your school as they long to meet you. Help them as they help you and you will find your way to new parts of the river.

75

REPLENISHMENT

We do not ask you to complete a certain amount of learnings every day. We simply ask that you take part and turn up; waiting to see what the path has to offer you that day.

On the path to enlightenment, we must replenish ourselves, with song, with love and with rest. We cannot expect to trek every day and not take a break. We must also remember that life continues to exist on Earth outside of the path and we must still play a part in that life.

While we may be on the path to enlightenment, others may or may not be. If we do not allow time to stop, rest and enjoy life our existence can be too serious, and this is not what we wish for you. There is a misconception that the path to enlightenment is hard and is a life of sacrifice. While it is hard and does require sacrifice, we are not asking you to spend all of your waking and sleeping moments on the path. Enter the path for the time you can allow each day and then retire from it at night and go back to your human life and sustain your human relationships.

The following morning or afternoon begin again. Your journey is as long or as short as you wish it to be because the path is about learning. Learning about the world, who you are and your place within it.

We do not ask you to complete a certain amount of learnings every day. We simply ask that you take part and turn up, waiting to see what the path has to offer you that day. Remember that you will not always know or understand the destination. Remember that you cannot see the twists and turns ahead as while you have a path to follow you do not have a map.

This is a journey of discovery and one that requires you to trust, with all of your faith and determination that the end destination is one you can reach. If you cannot trust that the path will take you where you need to go, then you may not be ready for the path.

If you require a map, then perhaps you have missed learning about the path itself. To know the path, you must trust the path. Not trusting the path is what will get you lost.

If you can trust the path, there will always be light up ahead. Some days this light will burn brighter than others. This is ok as long as you can still see it. However, be warned there will also be days where the light ceases to exist. These are the days you must trust the path the most and keep walking because too long in the dark will make you disillusioned.

Know that there must be days of darkness in order for you to be grateful when the light does reappear. Know that darkness can sometimes teach us more than light. Know that not all days come with a reward or a breakthrough. Some days are like walking through mud.

If you can trust the path, day in and day out you will eventually arrive at your destination. The path will not always feel good as this is the nature of a pilgrimage that ventures into your heart and soul. The path does not beckon us as it us who must commit to it. The path will be there whether we choose it or not.

76

LONGEVITY: PART 2

The path to enlightenment is the longest delay in gratification a human being can choose, therefore it is the most important.

On the path to enlightenment, you must embrace the longevity of it. You must know that the path is long, therefore your attention and commitment to it must be long also. If you see the path as being short, you will not last the distance. If you see the path as being long, then you are ready for a long journey, therefore are more likely to complete it.

If you tackle the path day by day, without a plan, you will run out of supplies and energy. If you plan for the journey taking the rest of your life (and potentially longer), you will pack and prepare for a journey that will take you the rest of your life. This is the nature of enlightenment. If you do not prepare, you will not make it to your destination. If you do not commit, you will not make it to your destination. If you are not prepared to lose your way on some days, you will not make it to your destination.

The path to enlightenment has many highs, many lows and everything in between. It is more hard work than fun, but it is more rewarding than a life of accumulation and illusion. Journeying on the path to enlightenment is about having a longer-term goal and being able to commit to something that is more than a lifetime, knowing that eventually, it will take you back to the sky.

The path to enlightenment is the longest delay in gratification a human being can choose, therefore it is the most important.

If you choose this path, know that it will be difficult and there will be some days you wish you did not choose it. The path chooses you. Sometimes our destiny takes us to the beginning of the path and asks us if we would like to take it. At that point, we are given a choice, and if we have guided you there, we hope that you will say yes. But saying yes does not mean it is guaranteed that you will make it to the end. We simply choose those who are most ready to take the journey and those who are closest to completing their time here on Earth (in lifetimes). The rest is up to you.

If you are committed, patient and kind to yourself and others, we will help guide you. If you begin on the path and you become selfish, impatient and unkind, the path will be a dark and lonely place for you. In this case, we would prefer you to be off the path than on the path as this is not a journey that strengthens the ego, it weakens it.

We understand we have not yet told you what is on the path. We are still preparing you for what it will take. If you want to undertake the most important journey of your life, is it not essential to know what to bring?

In time, we will share the path. In the meantime, we need you to decide if you are ready for what the path will bring, not just today, but tomorrow and in many years' time. If you are ready, we will continue with our preparation.

77

WATERFALLS

Each drop of water that makes up a waterfall is there because the right circumstances were created for it.

If we wish for a waterfall, we can either expect time to create it for us from tiny droplets of water or we can build it ourselves. Both are dependant on different timeframes. Both will bring a waterfall, but one may not be in our lifetime.

If we have an idea we are working towards and we wish to create it in our lifetime, we must bring the droplets of water ourselves. We must build the waterfall by clearing any obstacles it may have. This means clearing the path, finding the water source and then digging the tunnels by which the water will travel.

What the waterfall then needs is an edge or a cliff to drop off, and you must find this also. If you can do all of this, you will know you have a potential waterfall when the first drop of water falls over the edge of the cliff. You will know you have a waterfall when you see one. What you must remember is that each drop of water is purposeful. Each drop of water that makes up a waterfall is there because the right circumstances were created for it.

If you just wait for a waterfall to be created, it may not be. All kinds of environmental factors and conditions could permit the water to run in any other direction. So if you have a specific location or task in mind, then you best get planning on how to create the right circumstances, the right environment, and the water. It is by doing all of this that you can create the momentum you seek.

Do not wish for a waterfall as it may not appear. Work for the waterfall, and you have every chance of creating one of the most beautiful and free-flowing waterfalls in the world.

Life is what we create it to be, and it is by not giving up, by appreciating every drop of water, that we create the magic we seek.

78

CHAINS

Life and love without chains is possible for each of us, but first, we must know these chains exist.

In your life, there will be chains that will bind and attempt to break you. However, it is possible to break free of those chains if you are aware of what they are and what they are attached to. If we can see, feel and understand our chains we can see their source, and where they came from. Each chain has a lock on it, and as you know, locks can be locked and unlocked if you have the key.

As you spend time here on Earth, the chains you have acquired have been many. These are chains to objects, people, things, ideas you have about yourself and your place in the world. Each tie is a chain you are committed to and one you are also enslaved to. If you wish to free yourself, you must ask yourself why you allowed yourself to be chained up in the first place. You must ask why you allowed yourself to become the slave to someone else's ideas and ideals. You must ask yourself why you did not think you were worthy of being free.

This is something we are taught as children. As children we fight for our freedom and our right to explore, but as we grow these liberties are taken from us. As we grow, we lose the ability to see the chains, or we accept them freely as an exchange for love and whatever else we need.

For a chain, we may receive food or a job. For a chain, we may receive a relationship. What you must realize is that these chains need not exist and you do not need to be a slave to them. If you can be aware of this, you can see the chains as they are being drawn towards you and you can move away, disagree or find other ways of getting what you want and need.

Life was not meant to be led in captivity, for people, animals or plants. The chains that bind are also the ones that can set you free if you can find what unlocks them for you. The answers are all around you, just as hope is all around you.

Life and love without chains are possible for each of us, but first, we must know these chains exist.

Time does not set us free, but knowing that each of us has free will does. If we can lock ourselves up, we can also unlock ourselves from these commitments and ideas. Set yourself free as the path is so much slower and more painful when you are dragging chains. Know that you can only travel so far without unlocking the ties that bind. True freedom lies in never losing yourself to another.

The path we should walk should be beside each other, not as a slave to a master.

79

WILLINGNESS

To be willing with an open heart is what we wish for you here on Earth.

When we are willing, we can try anything. When we are unwilling, we close ourselves off to new situations, experiences, people and opportunities. Being willing comes with its challenges. To be willing is to be vulnerable, courageous, inquisitive experimental and free. To be willing is to engage without fear of repercussions.

If we can be willing to experience all that life has to offer, we can experience new ways of being and faster evolution. Why place roadblocks on the path ahead if we are brave enough to know barricades will be set there anyway? To expect difficulties is to be willing to overcome them. To be complacent and surprised when challenges arise is when we know we are unwilling to experience change. To be willing with an open heart is what we wish for you here on Earth.

If you are willing, you can be free. Free to experience life, love, pain, joy, and suffering. If you are unwilling, you will experience everything anyway but through a different, darker lens, a darker lens that will make you feel more like a victim than victorious.

Life will always present us challenges as this is what we signed up for. However, it is the attitude we use to face these challenges that makes us either willing or unwilling. If you can have a willing heart, mind, and soul, you will do well in this world. If you have a reluctant heart, mind, and soul, you will find many challenges during your time here, all designed to push you to be more open. What we often disregard is that the nature of life on Earth is to learn. When we are unwilling to learn, and learning is pain, we are missing the point of our existence. Therefore, open your willing heart to pain and suffering, but also to joy and openness and the road of life will be kind to you.

Be unwilling, and the road will naturally try to teach

you a lot, but it will be paved with obstacles. Open your heart to seeing life in a new way, and the obstacles will simply become what you overcome and pass along the way, not something that stops your progress altogether. Consider this and the path will already become clearer.

80

PROGRESS

Fall in love with the wandering, not the destination.

We know we are making progress when we are moving. What we must also grasp is that we are making progress even when we are not perceived to be moving.

When we are running towards something on the horizon, we can never seem to meet it. No matter how hard we try or how fast we run, the horizon we seek is always so far away. What we must recognize is that we can never reach the horizon as it is continuously changing. Just as the sun and the moon are always moving, so is the horizon. What we can expect is to meet specific landmarks showing our progress along the way.

Reaching the horizon is a beautiful dream we can

never catch, but we can still aspire to it. However, when our aspirations are never met, we can become disappointed. We can dream of the horizon, but if we measure ourselves on eventually touching it, we will become frustrated. However, if the horizon is the torch we run towards, experiencing different destinations along the way, the horizon then becomes a beacon of hope, leaving the places we encounter as wins we can celebrate. It is on the path where we grow, not reaching the end of it because it does not exist.

If the Earth is round, can we ever truly make it to the end of the Earth? We cannot, but we can find hope and peace in the times and experiences we've had circumnavigating it. This is the nature of life on Earth. We always dream of the end, finding the edge of the place we seek and a place to rest, but as soon as we think we arrive, the curve of the Earth continues, and we must keep wandering.

Fall in love with the wandering, not the destination. It is by being the wanderer and the explorer that you'll discover your true self. It is by learning who you are throughout the journey that you will grow. It is by being the person who is obsessed with finding the end and 'catching' the horizon that leaves us stagnant. Fall in love with the journey, the path, and love who you are on good days and bad because this is how you grow.

Life is not a journey with a planned destination. It is how many times we can circumnavigate the Earth during our time here that provides us with the greatest opportunities. It is our wins and losses that help us to know our true selves. Good and bad, beautiful and ugly, light and dark. This is life. This is love. This is you.

81

ENLIGHTENMENT

If you can accept that enlightenment means detaching from all that makes you who you are, then you are ready for it.

Enlightenment is when we wish for nothing more and nothing less. It is the complete peace that we seek, but it is also nothing.

When we seek enlightenment, we seek the joy we perceive enlightenment will offer. Except, this is not what enlightenment means. Enlightenment is not supreme happiness, it is the stripping away of all we rely on in the physical world. It is the internal world meeting the outside world and dissolving into one. It is nothingness and wholeness in a single breath. If you can believe that the path to enlightenment is possible, then you can also believe that it will and will not be what you expect it to be.

If you are wise, you will seek to strip back and merge your inner and outer worlds and not seek enlightenment itself. Stripping back for most people equals pain. Combining the inner and outer worlds means that we no longer need to put on masks when we visit the outer world. We are in perfect balance, but to find that perfect balance is painful.

No great leaps of growth occur without great leaps of faith. This is the way and it always has been. If you can identify that you need to grow, do not seek enlightenment, seek growth. Enlightenment is the by-product of many lifetimes of growth. To seek it, you must also understand and accept that you may never find it and if you do, it will not be what you expect.

We are not trying to discourage you from seeking enlightenment as there would be no purpose to this book. What we encourage you to do is not make this journey about the ego or about finding happiness. To seek enlightenment is to seek the path of pain. We do not climb without expecting to stretch ourselves mentally and physically further than ever before. If you are looking for a hill to climb, then enlightenment is not the journey for you. If you are looking for a mountain and accept that you may or may not reach the peak in your lifetime, then seeking the path to enlightenment may be what you are looking for.

Enlightenment is the complete sacrifice of all that you are in order to find all that you are not. It is growing and shrinking all at the same time. If you can accept that enlightenment means detaching from all that makes you who you are, then you are ready for it. If you can find it in yourself to seek a path that is unknown where there are no guarantees of success or failure, then perhaps you are ready for the path. If you can accept that this life may pass in the seeking of it, as it is more than a one-hundred-year journey, then perhaps you are ready for what the path will offer you.

The path to enlightenment is not quick. It cannot be achieved in thirty days, there are no 'tips' and no avoiding the pitfalls of the path itself. If you are ready to give up all that you are to become all you can be, knowing that this will not be valued in the physical world then perhaps now is the time to start.

The path and all of its grandeur is an illusion. The rewards it offers are spoken only by those who have never been there. Its pain is unspeakable and your faith in the path must be unshakeable. This journey is not for the faint of heart, but if you are drawn to it, perhaps you have already begun, not just in this life but in the lifetimes that have come before you.

Take your heart and your soul with you as this is all you will need. As you walk the path, you will grow and you will shrink. You will lose your faith and find it again. You will destroy the outer world to see the light of what lies within. Everything you have learned, you will unlearn. If you are willing to give up all that you are, then you may be ready to become all that you can be. Do not take this lightly as once the process has begun, there is no turning back.

MAGNIFICENCE

Life is too short to remain inside in your cocoon. Instead, embrace flight and the magnificence that flight offers.

When we heal and show our true colors, our strengths align with our purpose and we reveal our magnificence. When we allow ourselves to heal, we receive an indication of how magnificent we could be if we were not hindered by the pain of the past.

In our lives, we are like moths waiting to turn into butterflies. However, most people remain as moths never seeing the beauty of what could be because they choose only to live in the darkness and never break free. Living life in a cocoon is a dark place. Sometimes comfort can come from darkness because darkness is what we expect. For those who spend too long in the darkness, light and change can be scarier than living in the dark. It is only when someone wants light badly that they will find a way to break free. It is only through being willing to leave the darkness that light is possible. This does not mean a spark of desire to leave the cocoon, but a complete and overwhelming need to break free, which is something that can only occur when the moth has outgrown the cocoon.

We all outgrow our cocoons at some point, but sometimes we are unwilling to leave them as this shell is all we have known. Sometimes we turn into butterflies but never use our wings as unfurling them will mean flying. Flying can be as scary as leaving the cocoon. Most assume that when we transform into a butterfly that all of our problems are solved. This is not the case as being on the ground without a cocoon is still different to flying. Therefore, we must undergo a series of leaps and transformations, but without trust, we will remain the same.

If we are to become magnificent and free, then we must embrace flight, but first, we must embrace leaving the cocoon we have made our home. Safety does not equate to happiness or satisfaction, it equates to safety. It is only through risk that we achieve and only through flight that we will see the world from a different perspective. Just as fish swim in the sea and the birds fly in the sky, human beings must learn to use our legs and run. If we remain standing in the same spot, always dreaming of what could be, imagining how beautiful the mountains are, but never leaving our homes, then we are not using our legs.

If we are willing to leave our home and explore, even if we only travel a small distance initially, we can find our way and our wings.

Life is too short to remain inside your cocoon. Instead, embrace flight and the magnificence that flight offers. Embrace love, embrace light and know that even when you have transformed into a butterfly that you may still feel like a moth. To be a butterfly, you must see a butterfly. If your perception does not align with or trust your reality, then you will be miserable. Trust that life can be better, trust you have been created as a divine creature and trust that eventually your sight will catch up to your heart's desires.

Life is short, the sky is high, therefore do not waste time looking up into the sky dreaming. Take flight.

TRANSFORMATION

Remember that being lost can also help you find your way.

Over the course of this book, you have continued to evolve and change. As you finish each chapter, a new chapter opens for you. Each piece of advice, each wish that we have had for you helps you become who you are today.

If we look at transformation as a theme, it is the art of change. If your heart's desire is to transform, what is it you wish to transform into? Does the journey of transformation and not being tied to a specific destination allow you to fulfill your true purpose?

Is the journey one of being a moth that transforms into a butterfly, or is it that we are all butterflies, but we're learning to fly? This is what you are here to discover on Earth and each metaphor may mean different things to you and each time you read this book each metaphor may reveal itself to you in a new way.

If you are seeking the path to transformation, you must expect that this transformation will bring pain, just as life is pain. Do not expect that transforming from a moth into a butterfly will be easy, because in this process you are shedding your shell. And when the butterfly learns to fly, does it not fall first?

Life will bring you many ups and downs, but as long as you persist you will achieve growth. As long as you sustain yourself on the journey, you will continue to be able to travel the path you have chosen.

If you are the butterfly that falls and never attempts to fly again you will spend all of your life on the ground. If you are the moth that stays in its cocoon because it is safer, you will die because you cannot nourish yourself.

Life is full of pain and sacrifice, just as it is full of joy and gifts that only traveling this path can offer. Travel the path with a backpack that is light, but do not ever expect not to fall. Do not expect that you will never become lost, because being lost can be some of the most memorable and fulfilling parts of the journey. Remember that being lost can also help you find your way.

Life on Earth is as memorable as it is kind, as painful as it is joyful. Accept the path and all that it may offer you and you will lead a full life. Like all great movies, the storyline will have plot twists, highs, and lows. In life, we accept that all great stories present us with challenges. Do not seek to hide from the challenges life brings. Instead, embrace them and grow.

A tree does not grow and change without shedding its leaves and branches. The further you get along your path, the more mature and stable your trunk will become, and you will feel the loss of leaves less. Life is pain, but it is also joy. Life can and will be everything in between. Therefore, when you look for transformation, do not look for a destination, figure out how to fly.

84

INTRUSIONS

Learn to protect all that you value, but also know that if it is taken away, then life has something to teach us.

When something or someone intrudes, they interrupt our space and our time. Where interruptions are a break in time, an intrusion is more aggressive in nature, and it is not always welcome.

If we experience an intrusion, whether it be in our heart or our mind, we must ask ourselves why the intrusion has occurred? Where did this person or experience come from and what is it trying to wake us up to? Are we ignoring a part of our lives that we should be attending to more? Have we become lax about protecting ourselves, our space or our home?

Is there a guard down that should be up? Of course, we cannot be on guard all of the time, but the nature of an intrusion means there is a weakness there that needs addressing.

If you have experienced an intrusion lately then now is the time to rectify it. This can be across finances, career, relationships or security. What we must realize is that we can choose the intrusions we have, but if we did not choose them then a weakness exists. If a vulnerability exists, this is something to learn from and be rectified.

Learn to control your mind, body and your soul. Learn to protect all that you value, but also know that if it is taken away, then life has something to teach us. If intrusions occur, they have occurred for a reason. Know this, accept it and seek to rectify it. Everything that happens during our time here on Earth we can learn from. From the most pleasant experiences to the most unpleasant, there is something we can take from every situation. We are not saying that you must be grateful for every situation, we are saying there is something to be taken from all situations.

Further your own experiences, learn where your

weaknesses are and look to fill them in, but first look at why they are there in the first place.

FAITH VS BELIEF

Where belief is conditional, faith is unconditional.

Where faith is unwavering, belief can be lost. Faith can be lost too, but the nature of faith is that it is with us through rain, hail, and storms.

Faith is what keeps us getting up in the morning when bed is a safer, more attractive place to be. Faith ensures we give people an opportunity, even when others have let us down in the past. Faith is what moves people to act even in the most obstinate of situations when nothing seems possible or right with the world.

Faith begins with belief and transforms into faith when regardless of the odds or the options we persist. Where belief allows us to find the mountaintop of the cliff's edge, it is faith that helps us leap across the chasm that leads us to new places.

In our lives here on Earth, we will believe in and have belief in many things, but this does not always translate to faith. When we have faith in another human being, plant or animal, even when we are let down it is worth it. Belief is something we choose on a daily basis and while it can be strong, it is as easily lost as it is found. The difference between belief and faith is that faith can last a lifetime through all sorts of trials and tribulations and remain intact.

Having faith must be deemed worthwhile. Even on the darkest days, when everything we know, and we care about is being tested, faith is the ground that we stand on. It is the essence of what keeps us going. To move from belief to faith we must have an experience that deems faith worthy of existing. Faith is not something we choose, it chooses us and gives us the option to take part. We are then left with a choice, do we believe or not believe? If we believe, the next question is if everything in our life changes, could this be the one thing we can believe in and the one rock we can stand on?

Faith is belief that has been transmuted into the most powerful thing on Earth: freedom. Freedom from all that ties us down, freedom from the rain, the storm and the showers, freedom from the jobs we hate and the people that drag us down. Faith is perfection and perfection is perfectly imperfect. When others let us down, faith holds us up. Faith is love in the universe, but it is also love and belief in ourselves because the two go hand in hand. We cannot have faith without having faith in ourselves. Do you have faith in yourself? Or is this not yet possible? If it is not yet possible then what you have is belief.

Faith is backing yourself on the hardest days when you are carrying the most self-doubt, pain, and sacrifice. When you have faith you will know because nothing will shake or move it. Even when the whole world appears to be shaking and shifting around you.

Have faith and know that it will set you free. Have belief and be constrained to something that is dependant on time, places and experiences. What breaks belief is when others let us down. What breaks belief is when we let ourselves down. Faith is complete love, complete hope and complete faith that no matter what the universe brings, we will be ok and it is the divine vision for us. Life has many twists and turns, and with faith, we will always have the strength to carry on. Where belief is conditional, faith is unconditional. Find faith and you will find happiness even on the darkest days. Faith is freedom.

86

THE SKY

Love time, but know that it brings weakness and the weakness is that time is always slipping away. You cannot capture it and you cannot find a way or a technology to keep it as it is always going and never coming.

In the sky, we have no earthly desires. We exist to help others here on Earth. That is not our only purpose, however, we are also a go-between for other planes. When we speak of the sky, we speak of the place where you will go back to and where you began. However, it is some time before you will get here because your work on Earth is not yet done. It is just the beginning.

For much of our lives, we pursue a career and other things human beings think they should pursue. We get up, go to work, earn a wage and come home tired to our family or friends. By this time there is little left of us to share and little enjoyment, because how can one enjoy life when we are always tired? This is not the way, yet it is the way of so many human beings.

If human beings realized that the lessons they learn on Earth will eventually help them get back to the sky, they would treat their time on Earth differently. If they realized time on Earth is there to help them learn, then they would spend less time doing mundane tasks they do not love and instead work on what they enjoy and can be paid for.

There is no love in money or power and those who are in the sky realize this already as all is revealed on arrival here. On Earth, we forget everything we know and we must re-learn again. In time our knowledge begins to grow, but for so much of our time, we are distracted.

The Earth is in a state of chaos because we believe we are here for all the wrong reasons. We do not see our time here as a spiritual pilgrimage, we instead see it as a time to pillage. We pillage the Earth for her resources; we pillage our fellow man for his money and power, and we pillage ourselves when we give over too much of what we already can't afford.

In time, you will learn how little meaning most of what we do on Earth has on our overall life journey. If I were to give you a percentage, we learn on average only ten percent of what should and could be learning during our time here. What happens to the other ninety percent? It is wasted on illusions. Imagine what we could learn, perceive and take in if we shifted the focus to ourselves and our own learning from a young age? Imagine if schools were different and helped children uncover their purpose, not make them fit for an Earth that has already gone off track?

Imagine a life spent on love and spiritual fulfillment, where money and power did not matter and life and living were at the essence of everything? Too much time spent on work means we achieve little else. This is a shame because the Earth has much to teach us if we know where to look.

If you are reading this book, you must know that the answers you are seeking already lie within you. They are buried deep and covered with the residue of modern life. Everything you need to make you happy lies within you and in the environment around you. The time you have here is short, much shorter than what you would imagine and the time you have here will go faster than you could imagine. Therefore, do not waste time on what you know does not matter and instead spend your time on furthering your spiritual path, your happiness, what and who you love, and the rest will fall away.

Just as the sunset welcomes the night, so will the night welcome the day. The time you have here on Earth is all encompassed into sunrise and sunset. Do not waste the time you have as it is the only time you have in this body, this mind and this heart. You have been given this body for a reason, learn from it. Learn your purpose then fulfill it. See the future and your potential and pursue it.

Life is too short and too long to waste time. Like an hourglass where the sands are slipping away so is your life in every second. That time is not given back to you; it is merely loved and lost. Love time, but know that it brings weakness and the weakness is that time is always slipping away. You cannot capture it and you cannot find a way or a technology to keep it as it is always going and never coming. Do not take that for granted.

In the sky, you will remember all the lessons you

were destined to learn and understand you only achieved a few of them because you were distracted by the wrong things. This is an opportunity and a chance to re-focus. We are telling you how life works so that you can change your current path. Change your path, change the future and change your impact here. Do not waste it. Too many lives are wasted on the wrong things. Too many lives could change but don't. Too many lives passed away with regrets when they could have gone from this life to the next with more memories and lessons that mattered.

Seek your purpose now. Do not wait as waiting will never bring you what you seek. You must be active in your own life and learning. Learn as much as you can, strive as much as you can and do not be distracted by what does not matter. In time you will realize the impact you could have made but didn't. We pray this does not happen, but this is the way of Earth. We are giving you the answers now so that you may change your path, your existence, and your soul's journey.

If you are reading this book, you have an opportunity to be great. You are receiving the answers early, but you must use these answers to learn and change your ways. If you read this book and nothing changes, then you are not ready for the path to enlightenment. This book can remain a book, or it can be a map used to bring you all the joy you've ever wanted and needed, but only if you use it as it is destined to be used.

Time is not kind to us and knowing this should make you even more focussed on the goals at hand. Throw away what does not matter. Embrace all that does matter and spend time with who and what you love. Money and power only bring greed and greed will not bring enlightenment. The path to enlightenment is only for the pure of heart. Are you pure of heart, or do you have some more work to do yet?

COURAGE: PART 2

In the world we live in, we are encouraged to make change, but not make waves.

When we have the courage to speak up about our beliefs, challenges, desires, and fears, we allow others to come on the journey with us. When we remain silent, we allow others to stay silent too. It is only by having a strong voice that we can be heard, but some of the strongest voices are not working for the good of the world, but for the good of themselves.

In our lives, we will experience much diversity and sadness. We will see the human race try and fail in many different areas. We will experience the highs of achieving equality, and we will also feel setbacks where we lose hope that change is possible at all.

In the world we live in, we are encouraged to make change, but not make waves. This goes against the nature of making change, does it not? Why remain quiet about the causes and beliefs you are passionate about? Why remain silent when those who need speaking out for do not have the power to do it themselves?

In these times, we must stand up for each other and our rights to be a human race that values love. We must stand up for the love we want to see in the world and the hatred that must cease. We must challenge ourselves to rise higher than those who currently have a voice or a will to move against love. We must take the reigns of a planet and a people who have lost their way.

There is so much inequality on Earth right now. Isn't it time we tipped the scales back towards being a more peaceful and loving place? Life does not exist because of rules and right-wing opinions. Life exists because of love and love is what pushes us forward, so when you choose who represents you, choose those that serve and speak for love. Not one definition of it, but all definitions of it. Love at its center is pure, but love can become corrupt when those who crave power use it against those with weaker minds.

Love is powerful, but only when we give it power and a voice.

What the Earth needs now is love, not hate, so work for love, pray for love and speak out for love. Love will come when we find a way and the courage to overcome our hatred for ourselves and for those who are different from us.

CIRCLING BACK

We know to circle back when an issue that has been resolved sparks tension in the body and the mind.

When we are on the path to enlightenment, we may think we have learned all we need to know, but sometimes we must circle back.

The lessons we are learning are holistic, and where we may have learned them from one angle, there are other angles that may show the lesson is unresolved. In these times it is essential we reassess the lesson and look at it through a different lens.

The lessons you are learning go across many different lifetimes, and the ways you experience these lessons go across many lifetimes. So where you may have experienced a lesson as a young woman in one life, in the next you may experience it as an older man. This is the way. Know that each manifestation of the lesson may also have different angles that need to be explored in each body. For example, if you are here to learn the lesson of patience, then the patience you learn in your 20's will be different from the lessons you'll learn in your 30's and as your family dynamic changes. So do not see lessons as being fulfilled, as the lessons we learn never truly leave us. There are always opportunities for future lessons in each lifetime and it is important to consider this as and when these lessons arise.

We know to circle back when an issue that has been resolved sparks tension in the body and the mind. When tension is sparked, we must ask why and challenge ourselves to find the reason a lesson has re-appeared. Have we neglected to keep up what we had learned previously, or is this merely a case of a lesson continuing to reveal itself?

There are many lessons you will learn in each lifetime and across your many times, but there are some overarching themes that will be your primary focuses and challenges. For some people; it will be self-belief, for others; it will be self-love, trust, patience, determination, self-expression. Look for the broader themes as these are the ones that will take you furthest on your journey. Whilst these themes present your most significant challenges; they will also represent your greatest opportunities for success in all aspects of your life.

Know that if tension arises it is for a reason and should be explored. Know that if you are feeling pain then a lesson is needing to be resolved. Know that if a wound opens it needs to be tended to again to heal. If we are able to look at our grievances, tensions, and wounds as they arise, then we are empowered to keep moving along our path. If we let pressures build and wounds open without tending to them, it is only a matter of time before we collapse. Like first aid is for the human body, sometimes we need to stop and rest along the path to tend to our wounds. Do not place a band-aid on an open wound as this will not help it heal.

Diagnose the wound first, treat it and then continue to change its dressing as you help it heal. When you are strong enough again, you may continue. We cannot walk with open wounds, just as we cannot expect to heal without looking at what ails us. Remember this.

You can only walk the path if you are capable and willing enough to walk it, to overcome its challenges and to accept whatever the path may bring. If it is your lessons, then welcome them. If there are tensions in your life, welcome them. If wounds re-open, tend to them. You must repair yourself like a pilgrim repairs their body and mind along the way. Pushing through will not work as the path is long and may take many lifetimes. Consider this.

The path is kinder to those who seek to heal than to those who don't. Accept that healing is as necessary as rest. One cannot walk the path without healing one's wounds along the way. One can't reach enlightenment while they are wounded. This is both the challenge and the opportunity of walking the path.

REGENERATION

For a human to regenerate, first we must shed and be stripped bare. It is the stripping bare that is painful, the emptiness of when the last leaf has fallen that we feel naked; then we begin to feel at home with the nothingness that winter brings.

For us to regenerate, we must first shed. Think of the trees you see outside your window. Think of them in summer when their leaves are full and beautiful. Think of them in winter when their leaves are bare. What comes in between summer and winter is autumn and the autumn months are when trees shed their leaves and their stories.

What you must realize is that trees have their own personalities and their own journeys. They are not immune to change in the ways we think they are. It is just that we can see the process of their shedding and regeneration.

For a human to regenerate, first we must shed and be stripped bare. It is the stripping bare that is painful, the emptiness of when the last leaf has fallen that we feel naked; then we begin to feel at home with the nothingness that winter brings. After winter, spring makes its return, and we see our leaves start to grow again. We can choose to see the significance or insignificance of this process, and we can make it as major or as minor as we wish it to be.

If we wish for major regeneration, we must let all of our leaves fall until there is nothing left to lose. If we wish for minor regeneration, we can try and hold onto the leaves we still have, but they may be brown and lifeless. Therefore I ask you, what is the point of keeping ideas, hopes, thoughts, and dreams that no longer need to be on the tree of your life anymore? Why not shed them and leave room for new growth? The leaves have passed anyway. All that holds them there is you, they will not come back to life.

In your time here, you have been through this process many times before, but not to the extent you are willing to or must do now. You are beyond the point of no return. You are beyond coming back from where you are to where you were. The person you once were is but a shadow of an image of who are you are now. Let your leaves fall and do not try to cling to them as life sometimes needs to be lost to be found again. Just as the leaves disintegrate on the ground, so do your past ideas, beliefs and needs also dissolve.

If you wish for regeneration, you must accept there is a period of disintegration of the self. This is the most confusing time for a human being as there is nothing left to cling to or hold. Nothing left to hide behind, nothing left to hide your eyes and nothing left to look at other than yourself. Your leaves are what you cover yourself with. The trunk is who you are and even the trunk continues to disintegrate over time for fresh bark to grow. Who you are at a soul level lies in the roots you hide deep beneath the ground. Where the tree manifests in the way it wants to be seen with its leaves and trunk as changeable as the weather and seasons, what lies beneath is the truest sense of your desires and essence.

The answers to who you are do not lie in looking at the tree, they lie in discovering your roots. If you can go back to your roots, you can find out what you were before you became something in the world. The answers lie in what lies beneath, not above. When it comes to winter and you have nothing left to cover your tree, do not focus on the tree. Accept that what was there is now gone. Instead, look below to discover your roots as this is where both your truth and potential lies.

MASTERPIECES

You may leave your life as the beginnings of a masterpiece, with all the potential of a piece of marble or you can begin to chip away it, bit by bit.

We want your life on Earth to be a masterpiece of your creation.

We want the life you live to be the difference you want to make in the world. While we can aim to empower you, we cannot control you, and your destiny is not set in stone. Your life and your time here are written in sand and can be taken away at any time by your environment, the will of another or by death. The only certainty we can have in our lives is that you will have a life and an experience of life between birth and death. This is your time and what you choose to do with it is up to you.

When we speak of masterpieces, we wish to say that your life is crafted and polished over the time you are here. You may leave your life as the beginnings of a masterpiece, with all the potential of a piece of marble or you can begin to chip away it, bit by bit. Slowly carving and revealing a legacy you can craft for all of your days, leaving a memory of you long after you are gone.

If you do not complete your masterpiece, all you are left with is a piece of marble with potential. If you do finish your masterpiece, you can have a solid piece of work that represents your life, love, pain, and purpose.

Where are you at with your piece of marble? How far into the modeling of it are you? How many chips have you made to begin revealing its shape? Can you see yourself polishing it, or is there more time needed yet?

When you create daily, you are helping reveal the shape of your masterpiece, and over time it will become more refined. But what activities will help polish the marble? Where will you add the definitions that make it yours? See your daily work but also see your daily work as part of the whole masterpiece. If you can keep both in mind and work at it, you will finish what you started.

91

ENERGY: PART 2

You cannot change the amount of energy inside you, but you can shift it around.

You must learn to control the energy in your body, otherwise, it will control you. The rushes of energy felt during and after the awakening process are intense and you must learn to balance them. If you do not, they will work their way through your body at such an intensity that it may feel overwhelming or too much for the physical dimension your body resides in.

When you are in another dimension, the energy flows freely, but you do not live in another dimension. You live in this one. Therefore, you must learn to keep ascending while managing the energy as it does its work.

If you are noticing physical or energetic changes in your body, when you need to rest, rest. When you need to work, work. When you need to sleep and have an overwhelming need to do so, then you must do this. When the energy becomes blocked in a particular area of your body, then you must seek to distill it so that it may move again. You can do this through meditations, guided or unguided; this is up to you.

Imagine the energy in all of your body, scan it with your mind and realize where the excess energy is sitting. Once you have found this place, allow the energy to move freely to other energy centers or chakras where there may be a lack of energy. What you are seeking to do is balance the energy across all centers, not remove it. You cannot change the amount of energy inside you, but you can shift it around. This is a conscious effort though and one that requires you to check in daily as to where your energy is residing. Once you know this, you can change it. Like a see-saw, you can make the plank of wood sit flat.

In time and with practice you will be able to control the energy in your mind without meditation. You will notice an imbalance and move it with your mind. This will become more natural the more you practice it. These things take time and awareness. In the meantime, continue to read all you can about spiritual awakenings and the symptoms that come with it. In time you will learn to manage this process and not let this process manage you.

ENERGY AND MEDITATION

Life is like a river in that it carries those things to us that need to be dealt with, observed or taken into our mind or heart.

When you meditate, you charge up the body with energy. Meditation ensures a free flow of the powers that lie within you and allows you to tap into the sky and also the Earth. What this creates is a beauty that is unspeakable. A connection between mind, body, heart and soul, supported by the Earth and what lies above her, the sky.

If you can continue your meditation practice, your mind, body and soul will flourish as the energy connection and flow will only increase. The feelings you are left with after meditation can only increase as long as you continue to remove blockages along the way.

Do not fear the feelings that arise during meditation and whether they are right or wrong, just accept them as they are and let them float by like a stream carrying yesterday's news. If you wish to look at something, look at it for a second and then let it go. If it keeps coming up, accept it again and let it pass. There is no point fighting feelings or suppressing them because they will only continue to bubble to the surface.

Life is like a river in that it carries those things to us that need to be dealt with, observed or taken into our mind or heart. When we are releasing past experiences, traumas, thoughts or beliefs, the river can also carry these feelings away from us. Meditation is one format and one practice that allows us to do this and if we meditate daily, we will see significant results in both our outlook on the world and within.

Find a meditation practice you enjoy, one that makes you feel good but also tests you. The biggest tests we face often arise within the meditation, therefore learning the discipline you need to accept what arises and then let it go is what needs to develop in you. If you can do this you will experience significant effects. If there are thoughts that keep arising, this means that they need to be acknowledged like visitors arriving at your home. Greet them, welcome them in and let them go on their way again. Treat thoughts like visitors and know that while they are here for a time, they will not stay.

The thoughts we face will find a way to us no matter what, therefore isn't it better to have a way of working with them rather than against them? Find a meditation practice you love and you will reap the benefits. There are many different kinds and all are valuable in some way. Learn to work with them, try them out and see which one fits for you, but also know that your feelings may change tomorrow.
Enjoy life, enjoy meditating and accept who you are today, tomorrow and in the future.

93

TRANSCENDANCE

In between each breath, there is no breath and at that moment we are both living and dying at the same time.

When we transcend, we cross time and space leaving no doubt in our minds of who and what we are. When we transcend, there are no longer any questions about why we exist. There is simply existing and not existing, living and not living, dying and not dying. If we can tap into both ends of the spectrum, we can live as we were destined to live, with an understanding of both.

And when the reckoning comes we can know that we have given all that we have to be all that we are. And when the time comes to let go of all that we have, to embrace the nothingness of all that we are, when we return to the sky, we will know that we have transcended across time and space. We will know that we are space and we are time, and there is nothing in-between. If you can know this in your heart, there is nothing that can hold you back because what lies in-between the two worlds is love and an infinite nothingness. We are infinite nothingness disguised for a time in flesh and a personality. A mask that is designed to hide the person we are, were and who we will be. Embrace the nothingness within and you will find yourself, just as many have found themselves before.

Know that if you are kind to yourself and to the ones around you that you will be closer to who you are and who you will become. Know that the difference between life and death is a wish and an amount of time. Know that the actions of others can give life and take it away. Know that if you follow the light, you will arrive at your destination just as many others have arrived before you.

Take chances, take this chance that everything will be ok and you will find yourself. Take a chance on you and other people around you that you can find the destination you are looking for and that it lies in between death and life. In between life and death is where we live, constantly, every day. In between each breath, there is no breath and at that moment we are both living and dying at the same time. As we sleep and as we dream, there are moments when we are both alive and passed. From one breath to the next we can either be here or not here. This is the nature of life and death and both are a nothingness that we fill with something.

How we transcend is by embracing both and knowing that both take us to where we are searching for. Both take us back to the beginning which is, in fact, the end. Life begins when another life ends. Just as life ends as a new life is beginning. Transcendence is when we travel across time and space to join back with the nothingness of all that we can become for eternity or a day. This is up to you.

94

ENERGY EXCHANGES

By not paying the debts we owe, we can incur a debt far larger than the one we were originally needing to pay.

When we exchange energy with another human being, we give of ourselves so that they may receive a gift. In return we expect gratitude, but this does not always occur if the other soul does not see value in the exchange. To protect ourselves from this, we must only ever give our energy to those who are grateful to receive it.

We know those people by how they approach us, but even behind that approach is intent which is harder to recognize. Some people approach us with all of their cards on the table and we trust that if we do the same then the energy exchange will be completed and both parties will receive what they want.

When the other party does not reveal their intent then this is where a relationship or partnership can fall over as the approach can hide the true intentions of the individual who wishes to receive the gift. What the receiver does not realize is that by not finishing or paying back the debt they are taking on debt themselves. This will present itself as obstacles or blockages to abundance in their own lives. By not paying the debts we owe, we can incur a debt far larger than the one we were originally needing to pay.

We must always pay our debts as this is what upholds trust and loyalty in our society. If there is no trust and no loyalty then those with gifts will not share them and others will suffer because of this. If you have a debt, be sure to pay it. If you are the giver of gifts, then ask to be paid for the energy you give. If you are not paid you within your rights to ask for the debt to be paid. If the receiver still does not pay, then they may take on a karmic debt instead. If the debt is paid the obstacles will be removed, but the residue will remain. Only if the person truly learns from their mistakes will they be able to remove these debts completely.

This is the way of the universe and this is the way of energy. Those who owe you debts will pay them, but potentially they will need to encounter the repercussions of their debts before they do so.

EMPTINESS

Too often we mistake fullness for meaning, but there is no meaning in knowing too much.

To be full, we must allow ourselves to be empty. Emptying ourselves of thoughts, of free will, of existing is something that human beings are not practiced at doing but should be.

If we cannot empty ourselves, our cup will runneth over. A never-ending source of pain, of mistrust and busyness. If we can learn to empty ourselves of our pain, distrust and our busyness, our spirit can come forth and shine a light on what our purpose is and what we are here to do, but we can do none of this if we are too full.

From a young age, we are taught to collect food for our minds. We are taught to absorb information of all kinds. What we are not taught is which information is useful and which is not, because in the eyes of our teachers all information is useful. This is not true, nor has it ever been. Not all information is helpful, and not all souls require all the information on Earth to complete their earthly tasks. In fact, too much information can hold us back.

It is the stubborn naivety of not knowing enough that allows us to push forward with our hopes and our dreams, not the information that has been shared with us. If we knew too much we would never go, see or do anything. We would simply strive to absorb words, stories, truths, and untruths until our mind couldn't take it anymore. This is what we are on the road to here on Earth. All of the world's information lies at our fingertips, and the mistake we make is dipping in too often. Too often we mistake fullness for meaning, but there is no meaning in knowing too much. There is only meaning in the right questions and answers, but are there even any right answers as each soul's journey is ultimately unique?

These are all lessons we will learn here on Earth. These are all practices we must learn otherwise we will live in a distorted world forever, never moving, just absorbing other people's stories, words and ideas. Absorb ideas but know that they may always change. Do not build a wall around yourself and lock yourself in because you think you are right.

Be prepared to be wrong and be prepared that you must lose all you know to find the new ideas you may need. A traveller needs a map but the map doesn't define the journey, nor does the map explain the people you will meet along the way or the places you will visit. A map is two dimensional and you are five-dimensional, so stop using the map you have been given and throw it away as on this journey this map can no longer help you. You must help yourself. You must find yourself and un-find yourself. This is the only way.

Bless you, on your travels. Losing the map can often help you find your way.

96

LEAVING THE PATH

The path to enlightenment is there to challenge and reward us, but it can only do that if we have enough mental energy to give it.

Occasionally in our lives, the path becomes vacant for us or we become vacant in it. There are times in our lives when we must leave the path to know that we may come back. There are times when other callings in our life beckon us more than what the path offers. This does not mean that we can never come back.

The path to enlightenment is there to challenge and reward us, but it can only do so if we have enough mental energy to give it. When too much of our mental and emotional energy is being taken up elsewhere, it leaves little energy to walk, stroll and move along our spiritual path. We are not saying this is wrong, we are saying we understand that this happens for a reason and we will welcome you back when you choose this path again.

The path is always there as it has been for many centuries, but we cannot guarantee you will stay on it because sometimes our human form cannot cope with all that life brings us on Earth. We cannot strip ourselves back yet take more on. This is a puzzle that requires all of our knowledge, effort, and wisdom to maintain a life that is getting busier, yet attempting also to live a life of simplicity.

If you wish to re-join the path you can do so at any stage. The path never closes, it is never under maintenance and does not even close at Christmas. We are always here waiting to help you, but sometimes you only wish to help yourself. Sometimes human beings disregard our guidance in favor of their own. While this is human nature, you must accept that at times we have more knowledge than you. You must accept that at certain times, the path is a better place for you than the real world.

To stay on the path, you must be willing to listen to

us always. You must be willing to keep your spiritual practice, morning and night. You must be willing to meditate daily as daily meditation cleans and clears the mind, but most of all you must be ready to take on board the lessons you must learn. Life will not always present you gifts in traditional packages. Life will sometimes present you with a bomb that must blow up in order to free you from your cage. Accept that this bomb will come with pain, but also accept that it comes with growth and opportunity. Opportunity for a fresh start or to try something new.

If we know what we are doing and what we want, we can confidently walk the path and know we are going to get somewhere. If we do not have a destination in mind or we have lost sight of our original reason for joining the path, there will seem to be no point in continuing. Why put all of this extra stress on if it is taking you nowhere? But if you have a plan, a mission and something you are aiming to achieve, life on the path can be purposeful and pleasant.

Remember your reason for joining the path and it may facilitate you coming back to it again. Forget the reason you joined and you may never re-join.

Life on the path is not easy, but it is worthwhile. Fundamentally, we need a path in order to travel. At a soul level, we are traveling back to our roots and the place of our original meaning and birth. Find the path, and you will find your way home again.

97

HOLINESS

We are holy, we were born holy, but if we are not living a life of kindness, we are not living a holy life.

You don't have to be religious to be holy, but you must have good in your heart and your mind.

You don't need to subscribe to a certain way of living; you must only live well. Holiness does not occur based on a set of rules or recipes to follow. Living a holy life happens when we treat ourselves and others well, and we live with kindness in our hearts and soul.

The jobs we do will not make us more or less holy. They are simply jobs. Just as the relationships and company we keep will not make us holy either. Holiness is a way of living, and it is not attached to religion at all. Holiness is something we accept into our hearts when we are kind, loving and fruitful.

If you wish to be holy, then do not read books as books will not make you more holy. Do not dedicate your life to meditation or being a good mother or father. Instead, devote your life to being kind to everyone who crosses your path. We cannot know what people's intentions are, but we can always know that our intention is good and this is worth its weight in gold. The treasures that lie within us are not accessed by continuing to learn skills that are external to us. We are holy, we were born holy, but if we are not living a life of kindness, we are not living a holy life.

Learn to struggle and learn to heal and you will be kinder to yourself and others. Learn that life does not always go as planned and you will be kinder to others. Learn that life on Earth offers you no protection apart from the protection you give yourself and you will be more aware of your surroundings and the company you keep. Learn that life is never what we expect and only what we own and this will serve you well.

Life on Earth is an adventure and not a game. Life will bring us what we are ready for and what we choose to take on. Live a good life, a life of kindness and you will do well on Earth. We need more kindness and this kindness will set off a chain of events that may change the world.

98

PEACE

If we do not make peace with ourselves, with our lives, impact, potential and unrealised potential, we will never fully realise the role we were destined to play here on Earth.

Making peace with who we are and what our place is in the world is important. It is more important than anything we will do during our time here. When we make peace with ourselves, we accept ourselves for who we are, and we accept the changes we will need to make to become the people we wish to be.

If we do not make peace with ourselves, with our lives, impact, potential, and unrealized potential, we will never fully realize the role we were destined to play here on Earth. If you can learn your role, you can most certainly start fulfilling your place here. If you can learn your place here or the place you are destined to start at, then a new life can begin with you at the helm and your dreams on the horizon waiting to be reached.

If you disregard the role you have to play and instead focus on just living, then you will never realize the potential that could unfold for you if you were to give yourself the chance to fulfill it. Life on Earth is never empty and never full, it simply is and the sooner we realize that the better we are in ourselves and the better humanity will be for it.

We love each and every one of you not just for who you are today, but for who you will be tomorrow as well.

99

CHEMISTRY

Chemistry can light us up long enough to complete the current leg or the entire journey depending on how much we open ourselves up to it.

The chemistry we have with others cannot be controlled, nor should it. We can feel attracted to others, not through our current life, but through the many lives we have had with them before. Therefore, do not be afraid of chemistry, welcome it as it signifies the lives lost and the lives that we are still yet to live. We have been given companions on our journey to help us on our way. Chemistry can light us up long enough to complete the current leg or the entire journey depending on how much we open ourselves up to it.

If you believe you have been in a relationship with

someone in a past life, it is more than likely you have, and chances are you have been given this person again in this life. There are many companions you will meet along your journey that you have been with thousands of times before. Do not disregard this as they have been given to you in this life with a purpose too. Seek these people out, ask them why they think they are a part of your life and you will find the answers you are seeking. They may not remember the original reason they are here, but they will feel a connection with you also.

Life presents us with many challenges and with many people we have lived with over and over again. Familiarity is a sign of chemistry that has come before who you are now. Embrace it, love it and see where this chemistry takes you. In our lives, we are often destined to have many people we are connected with, and we should not be afraid of this because we believe life should be one way or another. Life should be as we wish it to be. Nothing more and nothing less.

Accept yourself, accept the attractions and chemistry you have and realize it is an indication of life that has come before that can now inform the present. We are here to live, breathe, love and take flight. The ones here with us are here to help us do that. Seek those who are familiar and you will find your way.

100

COMMITMENT

A commitment isn't the setting and achieving of a goal, it is setting a goal and knowing that you may spend your whole life trying to achieve it.

There are levels of commitment, each of them is important, and each plays a part.

When we think of commitment, we think of motivation and movement. We think of setting a goal and completing it. However, this is not the case. A commitment cannot be simplified to this extent. A commitment isn't the setting and achieving of a goal, it is setting a goal and knowing that you may spend your whole life trying to achieve it. It is understanding that when we commit, it may not be a linear journey or one we can track. Some of the most significant commitments we make are not measurable, nor should they be.

When we commit to our own development or the development of others, we are ensuring that we and the people we love or support will move further along their path. When we make a commitment to fulfill a dream, we accept that commitment will not define its success or failure, but it will help.

In our lives, we will make commitments that we can and cannot keep. For those we cannot continue, it does not mean our commitment was never there, it may just mean it was not achievable based on our own development or who or what lies around us. What we must aim to do is serve ourselves and others. If we can commit to love and all that love brings, we will live a good and worthy life. If we cannot commit to love or do not believe in it, we will lead a life of pain. Commit to love and this glue can last forever. Commit out of responsibility or duty and the glue becomes weaker by the second. Where love lasts, duty is only as strong as we are.

Commit to life, commit to pain, to love and to whatever the path brings you as you travel along it. Your levels of commitment are only as strong and developed as you allow them to be. You will only grow as much as you allow yourself to grow, unhindered and free. The moment you set yourself boundaries, conform or do something out of duty is the moment you begin to weaken.

Praise life, praise love and accept that the strongest forms of commitment are born of both. A life of love and commitment to it is one of the single greatest experiences on Earth. Enjoy it.

101

ANONYMITY

Express your thoughts, emotions and feelings for the world to see and you will capture the hearts and minds of all those around you. Keep your thoughts, emotions and feelings a secret, and you will forever feel trapped and bound by the opinions of those who do not matter.

When you are anonymous, no-one can learn from you. When you keep your thinking and your learning a secret, how can you expect yourself to grow? There is nothing to be ashamed of in finding your spirituality and connecting back to it. It is something to be ashamed of when you cannot express your thoughts freely without fear of reprimand.

In the world we live in today, there are many people

who can't share their thoughts, feelings or what they've learned about the world by living in it. It is a shame that we cannot all express who we are and who we want to be without worrying about what the world will think of us. When we have fear in our hearts and our minds, we become smaller until eventually, we die out.

Express your thoughts, emotions, and feelings for the world to see and you will capture the hearts and minds of all those around you. Keep your thoughts, emotions, and feelings a secret, and you will forever feel trapped and bound by the opinions of those who do not matter.

We must create a world where bravery is rewarded, not beat down. We must create a world where having an opinion, a voice and a way to share it is celebrated. We must reward and support those who are brave enough to put themselves out there, even when it means losing everything they had before. This is important, what counts and what we must move towards.

The world needs your voice, your way, and your opinion, so don't hide it. There is no value gained by hiding who you are and what you stand for. The world needs you more than ever.

WHOLENESS

Don't make the mistake of walking someone else's road. Pave your own, make it yours and the road will always lead you to where you want to end up.

We do not feel whole until all of our pieces are put back together. The challenge with this is that we are never whole until we come back to the sky. It is the moment we come back when we feel whole again. Therefore, is there any point in chasing wholeness when the beauty of life is accepting it for its imperfections?

Life will never present a completely smooth road, but it can present us with one that is enjoyable to travel. If we learn to love the bumps, the breakdowns, the burnouts, and the beauty, we can learn to live in a way that sets the right expectations.

Movies make us feel like life should be perfect, but there is no perfection, only imperfection.

It is in our imperfections, our moments of grief, sorrow, and pain that we are most beautiful and most pure. It is when we are not curating the masks we wear or faces we show that we let our true selves shine. It is only through understanding the road we travel that we understand the point of traveling at all. It is only when we see the destination do we understand all the roads we can take to reach it. Life is a journey as people say and the beauty of the journey is to take all of it into your heart and mind. Do not leave anything behind. Do not break for those who wish to break you. Do not get so beaten down by life that you stop the journey altogether. If there is a will there is a way and the way is forward.

Life will present you with many challenges, but now is not the time to give up. Now is the time to gather all of your strength and put your best foot forward. Now is the time to keep smiling throughout the showers and to say 'I've got this', even when you feel like you don't. A new road is not all paved at once, it must be paved one step at a time, and this is what you are doing. Don't make the mistake of walking someone else's road. Pave your own, make it yours and the road will always lead you to where you want to end up.

Life is a challenge but it is also a joy, we just need to know where to look. Thank you for continuing to travel and bring others with you. We will continue to shine a light on you so that even in the darkness you will know your way.

Take this time to take stock of who you are, where you have come from and what you wish to do next. You have come a long way and there is a long way to go, but you will reach your destination if you continue traveling. Be safe, be strong and be true. Life rewards travelers.

103

INVESTMENTS

If we can invest in ourselves and garner support for what we care about, then we have a genuine chance at changing the world.

When you invest in yourself, you invest in your future and your place on this Earth. When you do not invest in yourself, no-one else will either. Some may confuse investing in yourself with arrogance or self-interest. This is not the case. There are of course those who are arrogant and self-interested, but these people can be seen from a long way away.

For those who invest in themselves who are genuine, kind and giving, there is endless abundance and support from those who love and respect you. Therefore, do not see investment as self-interest, see it as self-love.

If we can invest in ourselves and garner support for what we care about, then we have a genuine chance at changing the world. If we can act from a place that is humble, but still be brave enough to ask for support, we can make the difference we seek. If we can find a home for our work and our passions, a home that is supported by love and wealth, then our opportunities are endless. People want to invest in those making a difference, therefore do not hide what you are working on, celebrate it. Shout it from the rooftops and do not be afraid of those who may see it as self-investment as they are afraid to do it themselves.

Act on your interests, your passions and help the world become a better place. Not because you need to, but because you want to. Leave your assertions behind and practice self-love. Show others how to do that too. Self-love is important, saving the Earth is important and anyone brave enough to be in the ring deserves support.

We love you.

104

HOPE: PART 3

Hope is the sun lying on the horizon; hope is the calm waters in a stormy sea and hope is the love we still have in our hearts when the world has beaten us down.

Hope is the friend we never give enough love to, yet hope is the friend who sustains us and gives us life. Hope fuels our dreams and staves off our nightmares. Hope gives us strength when we have nothing left, even if it just a glimmer or a crack. Hope tells us to keep going when there is no rhyme or reason for the unrest in our lives. Hope gives us the opportunity to change and to keep growing, even when we believe we are an old tree that has nothing left to give.

Hope is what makes us who we are and reveals the

best elements of ourselves. Hope is who we are at our core and the center of our being. Without hope we are an empty shell, waiting for the wind to come and breathe life and sound into us.

Hope is what we need, yet we often do not have in our darkest moments. Until a little crack of light bleeds through and we can see the light, even if it is just a sliver in a world of pain and regret. If we can hold hope and feed it, hope will look after us and see us through. If we can nurture hope, hope turns into new life, new opportunities and new growth.

Hope is the sun lying on the horizon; hope is the calm waters in a stormy sea and hope is the love we still have in our hearts when the world has beaten us down. Have hope, find hope and when you do find it nurture it like a long lost lover or friend and be grateful for its arrival because once hope arrives, it never leaves. Sometimes it is just hidden.

105

WORK

Work should not feel like work, it should feel like play. And if it does feel like work, then we have not yet found something synchronous to our soul.

When you work, you switch all other parts of yourself off. When you work, you trust that the work you are doing is for your highest good. Or potentially you know it is not for your highest good, but you hope it will take you there nonetheless.

Mindless work is not good for anybody, just as being unhappy at work is not good for us either. When we are happy and feel fulfilled at work, we are free. The work frees us and does not constrain us. This is the goal we must work to with our life's work. Work should not feel like work, it should feel like play.

And if it does feel like work, then we have not yet found something synchronous to our soul.

Finding what is synchronous to our soul is easy if we can allow ourselves to ask and also to know it is ok not to have all the answers.

When we are free, we experience profound moments of intuition and serendipity. When we are constrained, we have hope and can see a possible light up ahead, but we are not free to pursue it. Yet when we are doing our life's work and the work that is aligned with our soul, we are free to pursue the light and the synchronicity whenever we please.

Find joy at work and in your work, and you will find freedom. Just as many have done before you. For the parts of your work that you do not enjoy, release them and focus on what you do enjoy. Life rewards those who chase what they are seeking at whatever cost. Life will feel full for those who make it full. Life will feel empty for those who feel empty inside.

Maintain your strength and find your courage to pursue whatever lights your soul on fire. A candle will only get you so far.

106

BURSTS OF ENERGY

When you have a burst of energy, like a boat uses the wind in its sails, push further and make the most of a strong headwind.

When you feel a burst of energy, you feel renewed and restored. When you are lacking in energy and are fatigued, it's like you are walking through thick mud or sand. Neither is right or wrong. Each is about knowing when you go slowly and when to move with the speed of the wind.

When you have a burst of energy, like a boat uses the wind in its sails, push further and make the most of a strong headwind. When you are feeling sluggish and slow, know that your body feels it needs rest and it is wise to take this rest before your body collapses.

In today's culture, we are taught that we must always be 'on', twenty-four hours a day, seven days a week. The body was not built for this, nor was our mind. If you are wise, you will take the advice and the signs of your body as a barometer for when you push and when to pull back. Your body is the best indication you have of whether it is time for work, rest or play. If you ignore the body and the signs it is giving you, you risk having a forced stop in your day, week or month.

A forced stop is when the universe sends you a stronger than usual sign that it is time for you to retreat. This can come in the form of sickness or even an injury, depending on how strong the message needs to be and how little you listen. Some stops are stronger and longer than others. If you wish to avoid this, you would be wise to heed the warnings your body is giving you before a stop like this is incurred.

If we are wise and in tune with our body, we will realize that it works in ebbs and flows, with and without force, with speed and without speed. We cannot go fast all the time, nor should we. All people need days off in their minds and their bodies. To ignore this is to ignore the signals of the body you reside within. We are given limitations for a reason and we should be mindful of these.

Sleep when you need sleep. Rest when you need rest. Play when the world weighs too heavy on your shoulders and laugh when the world becomes too serious for you. There is an antidote to everything, but we must be in tune with ourselves to know what that antidote is.

You will always get everything you need done. It is just some things take longer than others, but all things will take longer when you are tired. Therefore rest and then try again, whether that be tonight or tomorrow. The time we have here goes quickly and slowly depending on how we look at it. Know there is time for rest, time for play and time for work. Time overspent in one area neglects another and this is where we run into problems. Seek to nurture all three and you will lead a good and happy life.

107

DESTINY

Time will not give us extra time because we beg or ask for it. Nor will it bend to our needs or wishes.

When we believe something is destiny we are less likely to make it happen. When we express our destiny as a thought or as an action, it is more likely to come to fruition. So much of our human lives is spent in worthless pursuits that neither take us here nor there. Yet if we could channel our energy into a purpose, a place, or creating something magical, we would be proud of what we achieved and it would propel us forward.

Instead, we spend our time focussing on what does not matter which leaves no space for what does. If we can dedicate our time and our attention daily to creating something for the future, there will come a time to relax, but that time is not now. There is too much to see, too many places to go and too much work to be done. Imagine your time here as sands within an hourglass. Eventually, that time will run out, whether that will be by natural or unnatural means.

We cannot predict when our lives here on Earth will end; therefore we should aim to make the most of the time we have. If we do not, we will only experience regret at what we have lost and what we never found. Time is not our friend, nor our enemy. Time is just time. It is what it is, and it also is what it is not. Time is something we do not control, nor should we try to. Time will not give us extra time because we beg or ask for it. Nor will it bend to our needs or wishes. Time and our time here is the only thing we cannot predict, yet it has the greatest amount of control over us. If we can look at time the way we look at our loved ones we would cherish it for its strengths and weaknesses, its quirks and its strange ways of operating. We would love it on its good days and its bad, and we would cut it slack when it took a bit more than we'd have liked it to.

Life on Earth is our greatest mission, accomplishment and what we all live for. But sometimes we forget to live and all we do is waste time. Do not waste the time you have, just as you should not waste the time you have with the people, places, and creatures who love you. Time is not to be laughed at, missed or mistreated. It is to be respected for all it gives and all it takes away.

Respect time and respect the time you have left in this body, in this skin on this day. Make the day yours, enjoy the night and love every minute as once it is gone, it will never return.

108

ABANDONING THE PATH

No mountain peaks were ever reached by taking a slow walk around the block.

When we abandon the path we are on, we are walking away. It does not mean we cannot or will not come back, but it does mean we have become disillusioned or disinterested in the path. This is not something we can change as nature, and our thoughts, feelings, and emotions must run their course, but we can wait it out.

Waiting it out can be done in many different ways. We can simply sit and wait for a light bulb moment to come, but this is often unfruitful and wastes time. We can contemplate following a new path and see if that sparks our interest. Or we can contemplate why we left the path in the first place and try to understand what prompted this exit and how we can seek to get ourselves back on track. When we lose focus, we begin to drift. Often we need to leave the path in order to know why we need to get back on it and the speed we need to operate at in order to regain lost territory and time.

When you have left the path, always know that it will welcome you back when the time is right. When you have begun a new path, know that the old path is always there waiting for you if you choose to return. If you choose to abandon all paths, know that new paths can be made if your feet are tough and you are willing to walk your own way. Walking your own way is not easy, but it can be very satisfying and provide the most insights and interesting travel stories.

We are not here for a long time, therefore we should make our journey and our travel worthwhile and enjoyable. No mountain peaks were ever reached by taking a slow walk around the block. The most beautiful views are experienced after the most horrendous and trying of walks and this is what we must remember. When times get tough, remember that no great feats from humankind were ever created or experienced by being lazy or by idly strolling to our graves. All of the greatest feats, accomplishments, and acts of grace were created under the pressure of self with the drive of no-one else but you.

Life will not urge us to complete our greatest wishes and dreams, but it will remind us that time is short as those around us fall and get back up again. Time travels faster than we will ever realize but slower than we will ever dream if we are not following our true path. If you can be brave enough to take a leap of faith, climb your own mountain or travel the path less traveled or not traveled at all, you will achieve more than you could ever imagine. The blood, sweat, and tears you will experience along the way are simply tokens and remembrances of your journey. Love these tokens as much as you love the experience and joy of reaching your destination. Both are important and are to be cherished.

Walk with pride, but not too much pride that you lose your way. Walk with heart, but not so much heart that when you fail you cannot cope with the weight of that failure. Walk with hope, but not too much hope that you believe everything will be delivered to you on a silver platter. Life is to be experienced, cherished, managed and embraced daily. Anything less and we are drifting aimlessly on a pond with no destination other than eventually hitting the shore.

Travel the lake, but be ready to leave it for the ocean when the time arises, a place where you can float and swim wild and free. The ocean is where all of our desires lie, but we must be willing to leave the safety of the lake to experience what life in the ocean can bring.

INTERESTS

Money comes and goes, but the richness of your heart can only be filled with experiences, love and hope.

What we are interested in defines us. What we spend our time doing makes us who we are, but there is a difference between what the world expects and pays us to do and what we are truly interested in and passionate about. What we must learn to do is strike a balance between the two. What we must aim to do is learn to conquer and manage both, knowing that one feeds the other. However, the ultimate goal is to pursue only what we are interested in.

If you think of Earth as a giant school, would it not be better for us to pursue what we are interested in versus engaging with a curriculum that was not built for us? Would it not be better for us to lose more money and less time and pursue what we love, what we adore and what we can see ourselves doing for the rest of our lives? Money is not everything as we know, but a strong and engaged heart can bring us so much joy.

In time you will be in a place where you can pursue only what interests in. In time, after you have paved this way, this journey, you will discover that the place you have landed in is the place you have longed for, dreamed of and hoped for. In time you will see that the bravery you have had in leaving your established path has allowed you to pave a new path, a new way, and a new life for yourself and your family. If you had not done this you would be rich in your possessions, but not in your heart. There you would be poor and would always be longing for this path, but it would not be one you had ever paved.

The bravest thing we can do in our lifetime is pursuing what makes our souls happy and what interests us. We can ignore our interests, what and who we love, but it is only us that is poorer for that. The world does not care what we pursue, but we believe it does. The world does not care how we make our money, only how much of it we do make. Therefore, if you can learn to live to a certain standard, but not be dependant on money, then you can be the freest man or woman on Earth. Learning to live without money and not be dependant on it is a freedom that most will never experience. Even if you can make a little from your craft and substitute it with money from elsewhere, you will be so much happier than following a dream that is not yours.

Remember this when you have no money in your bank account, but you are rich in your heart. Money comes and goes, but the richness of your heart can only be filled with experiences, love, and hope. And what you build in your heart for yourself can never be lost, traded or found in the heart of another.

What you have in your heart is yours, and that can never be taken if you build yourself to be bright and strong. Believing in and following your interests is the pathway to a long and happy life.

110

REDEMPTION

We can only be free if we know what still chains us and this can be found in the lives and times we have chained ourselves to, in a mind that cannot remember and a soul that cannot forget.

On the path to enlightenment, we cannot expect others to travel with us, just as we cannot expect others to endorse our journey. The path we travel is not for all and all will not wish for us to travel it either.

There are those around you who will wish for life to remain the same, forever stuck in a time warp where every day is the same and nothing ever changes. There will be those around you who will be happy for you to change and evolve but only in the realms of what they deem possible. For these people, any sudden growth will set off alarm bells. There are those who say they want you to reach the peaks of Earth's highest mountains, but they will only want you to reach the top of the molehill. All of these people will exist on your journey and you must expect to face all of them.

The last type of person you will encounter will tell you that you are not qualified to travel this path. They may say that you are not smart enough, or that you have not read enough books. They will say you have not travelled to the most spiritual places on Earth or that this path is not your birth rite.

The path to enlightenment does not discriminate based on age, ethnicity, gender or anything you have done in your past. We do not believe the past defines the future, but we do know you must be capable of sustaining yourself on the path long after the final rays of sunlight have gone down and the path is lonely and empty.

To stay on the path in all weather, you must prepare for all weather. To last day after day, never stopping, you must prepare for a life where very little gratification exists.

The reward of travelling this path lies not in the

congratulations of others or special powers, but in knowing that you are working towards your spiritual fate. To know that you are tying up loose ends from lives gone by and that you are happy to put yourself and your wishes aside to help others. It is the least congratulatory path of all paths and no-one is waiting for you at the finish line except yourself as you are the sole competitor and the creator of this race.

In time you will come to understand that it was never about anybody else. It was about you and you only. It is through facing your demons and your fears that you will travel further along the path when others decide to turn back.

People mistake the path for being one that mystics and spiritual masters walk, but really it is a path back to our own redemption. It is not walking forward; it is walking back across all of our lives and tidying up the mistakes we have made, the lives we took in battle or otherwise and resurrecting who we were before we lost our way.

When spiritual masters say it is not a discovery, it is a remembering; this is what the path to enlightenment is all about. We cannot become someone new by not acknowledging who we were and who we are now.

Life does not promise us rainbows, but it does give us the opportunity to be free. We can only be free if we know what still chains us and this can be found in the lives and times we have chained ourselves to, in a mind that cannot remember and a soul that cannot forget.

The path to enlightenment is not golden every day. Some days it is fraught with danger, sadness and the grief of who we were before we were conscious. It is only through embracing that shadow side that we can truly love ourselves.

111

MISSTEPS

If you are wise and know that each step is a step forward, the destination on the horizon is always moving closer.

When we make a misstep, this is not something we should beat ourselves up for. Life can only be predicted one step at a time, therefore, how can we know what lies ahead if we cannot yet see the destination? A misstep is not a mistake, and it is not a step in the wrong direction, it is a step in a direction, and this is all that the spirit world can hope for.

When we ask you to push forward with your pursuits and your interests, we do not do this because we are harsh tutors and only want you to succeed. We know that momentum only comes with movement and movement is what will make the difference between reaching your destination or destinations versus not going anywhere. A misstep is still movement and this is why we celebrate the missteps as, after all, they are just steps in a direction.

On your travels, do not ask if you are stepping in the right direction. Instead, use your intuition and keep moving, day by day, hour by hour and minute by minute. Every step is a step forward and one you should be grateful for and proud of. Giving ourselves a hard time for our mistakes and our missteps does not help anyone, it hinders us.

If you are wise and know that each step is a step forward, the destination on the horizon is always moving closer. If you make what you deem to be a misstep, you must simply move to the next step. Just as a frog leaps from lilypad to lilypad, there is no 'wrong' lilypad for the frog. It is merely another lilypad.

Human beings, like frogs, are all trying to make their way in a world that sometimes does not make a lot of sense. A world where rhyme or reason sometimes does not exist. It does not mean that the world is wrong, it means there is a bigger picture we do not see yet.

112

ELEGANCE

What we seek for you to realise is that when you are doing what you are born to do, the layer that coats your body becomes thinner and you are closer to spirit.

Elegance in our work allows the beauty to shine through. Whatever we do or turn our hand to, to do it to the highest level of our ability is beauty. When we are channeling our soul from the skies above, we are showing our elegance.

When we were stars, before we were born, we were elegant. Yet when we arrived in our human form, there was an element of ourselves that arrived unable to move as freely as we'd wish to in our bodies. There is a clumsiness that comes with being in the human form as the spirit is far bigger and more powerful than the human body allows, which is why the spirit must shrink while it is in human form. This is not something we account for or are aware of. We simply feel that we do not fit.

When we do not fit, our actions do not match the images we have in our minds. If we speak of surfers, when we are able to surf at a professional level, the surfboard and the human melt into the wave, riding seamlessly across the water's surface. The surfboard uses the water to gain speed, but it is not part of the water. Just as you are not part of the Earth, but the Earth can amplify your abilities and make you bigger than what you are.

When you look at your talents, think about what makes you feel clumsy or like you do not fit. Now look to the tasks or projects you do that are effortless and where the Earth is merely a launchpad for something greater moving through you.

For some human beings, it may be sport or the pursuit of pushing the body as far as it may go so that they may reach the spirit. For others, it will be art that allows them to touch spirit. For some, it may be music and when their fingers hit the guitar strings, there is a melody or tune that breaks through which the soul has heard before. Some may write, some may sing, some may use their mind to push to great places.

What we seek for you to realize is that when you are doing what you are born to do, the layer that coats your body becomes thinner and you are closer to spirit. When the body is not allowed to get in the way but is instead used as an art form in itself, you will feel the water of the Earth pushing you along the waves and you will simply move with the changes in your life. If in life you feel like you are being drowned with wave after wave crashing over you, you have not yet found the tool or the surfboard that will help you release yourself.

When you let the Earth hold you and propel you, you are more you than you are on any given day. When you allow the Earth and its mystical properties to support you and create a trail, you will never become lost, you will simply move further towards your goal.

When you are the surfer and you allow the waves to be your friend and not your enemy or something to fear, you will be closer to heaven and still remain in the form you are in now. Express your body, express your spirit and allow yourself to be free. This is what we have always wished for you.

113

FRUGALITY

In our lives, we will take many risks, but we never risk losing our identity until we embark on the path to enlightenment.

When embarking on a new adventure, we must be frugal as we do not always have the luxury of money to support us.

When the road of our life takes us down a new path, one of our choosing, we must be prepared to sacrifice all that we are and own to find a new version of ourselves. Truth be told, it is not a new version, it is just a version closer to who we really are.

To be light enough to take a leap of faith and to see where it takes you, you must not have any constraints holding you down or tying you up.

Can you imagine trying to leap from one side of a cliff to another with a rope still tying you to the other side? How can you venture on when one rope still binds you to who you were before? You cannot. Therefore, you must be prepared to leap without a rope and often without the financial means to support you in the way you feel most comfortable.

The trouble with comfort is we do not move anywhere near the rate we need to. As card players would say, we need to have some 'skin in the game' for the game to proceed at the rate and rapidity we wish for. To have skin in the game is to take a risk.

In our lives, we will take many risks, but we never risk losing our identity until we embark on the path to enlightenment. It is here we are asked to leave who we are behind which is the most significant risk we will ever face, yet on the path, we will do it many times over as who we think we often just mask another layer underneath.

The first shedding of our identity is the scariest; after that, it merely becomes another face, another name, another job and another lifestyle we lose. It is very much a similar process to what occurs in reincarnation. Each time we are born, we are born into a new body. Each time we die, we leave this body to go to our next one. The identity changes we experience in this life are the same. As we lose one identity we have created, another reveals itself.

You may ask why we cannot move straight to spirit? The reason for this is that if you are on Earth, you still need a human form to operate within. People could not relate to you if you were simply spirit.

You may now wonder what the point of shedding more of your identities is if you can never get to spirit? We did not say never; we said you needed to retain an element of your humanness so that you can touch the lives of others.

What this constant shedding of identities requires from you is the ability to live on as little as you need to pursue this path. If you are committed to an identity, socially and financially, how will you ever release it? It is only through being nobody that we can become somebody, only to discover that the more we are nobody, the happier we can become. It is through being fluid and being able to shift between the stages of our unveiling personalities and appearances that we can get closer to who we truly are.

Not being financially committed to a certain lifestyle

allows you to pursue the path and the adventures you will have along the way. Perhaps as one identity shifts, a new one who loves travel is revealed. We understand you need money to travel, but money can be attained in many different ways and we do not need a set of chains attached to us to earn money. The more transient you can become, the freer you are to pursue the lessons you need and wish to learn.

Set yourself free from the ties that bind and earn as you need to. What you will realize is that what you think you need to live can be freeing if you live frugally, but can be a burden if you believe you need more than what you earn.

114

WISDOM

What is right for the pig is not right for the cow and what is right for the butterfly is not right for the snake. We all need different types of wisdom and teachings.

When we have wisdom in our hearts, we acquire elements of ourselves needed to be free. When we are wise enough to recognize what is missing or what needs to come and go for us to be free, we will either acquire or release it.

In time, if the path is clear and we allow ourselves to be wise with our own decisions and our own hearts and not let our lives be run by others, we will find what we are looking for.

In the life and times in which we live, many people presume themselves to be wise, but all they hold is information. Wisdom is having knowledge, but knowing when and where to apply it. It is knowing what strength to apply to something and when we do in fact need to back off. It is knowing when we are pursuing something we should not and knowing when our soul craves more.

When you are wise, you will make good decisions, but these decisions will only be the best decisions you could make at the time as foresight is not something available to you unless you have connected with the sky. And even then, what can you expect to see when the world is constantly changing?

Every person on Earth has wisdom within them as it applies to the experiences they have had in their own lives. One person cannot presume to be wiser than another as we have not had all of the experiences on Earth. A mother in Venezuela may be wise in her hometown, but she may not be wise to the ways and times of living in another foreign city as someone who works in banking. We all have different experiences and wisdom to offer, but what you may wish to offer may not apply to all people. What is right for the pig is not right for the cow and what is right for the butterfly is not right for the snake.

We all need different types of wisdom and teachings. We must seek out those teachers who can help us learn how to fly, run on the ground or whatever our interest may be.

Wisdom can be shared, but it can also be dissipated when the decisions we make erode the knowledge we once had. Just because we were wise in the past does not make us wise in the future. The nature of wisdom is that it is built on experience and our experience is constantly changing. Therefore, what we were wise in yesterday may not be the same today, and we can openly admit this.

You could say 'Yesterday I knew this to be true, but today I am not so sure as the world and its people are continuously changing'. What we have learned is not the be-all and end-all and learning does not ever stop. This is why the idea of being a scholar is so challenging. It is a role that is continuously being earned. Just because someone was a scholar yesterday does not mean they are one today as the knowledge they had yesterday may not apply today. The nature of a scholar is to learn constantly and this role should be celebrated if the scholar does continue to learn and not become stagnant.

In our lives here on Earth, we cannot presume to

know all, see all and be all. In a minute or a second, we can presume to know something and be wise in it, but we must be open enough to know that wisdom expires and must be kept up, maintained and managed. When old wisdom is no longer relevant, it must not be held onto. It must be let go to make room for new knowledge, which can be transformed into wisdom.

Do not presume to be an expert in a space. Instead, aim to know all you can and be a learner who aspires to learn forever. We cannot presume to know mountains just because we have climbed one. To know mountains, we must climb them all and this includes volcanoes because they are mountains too. What we must aspire to is evolution and we must embrace all thoughts and opinions, as each may help us create our own. We can then choose what to keep as knowledge, when to let go of expired information and what we wish to turn into wisdom.

Life is a never-ending circle of growth and there is no end. Be a life learner and you will find your way to the finish line, only to begin again when the time is right. Life is growth and growth does not have a stopping point. We are always in a state of regeneration and dissipation. It is when we allow ourselves to dissolve that we can grow into something new.

AGONY

We cannot avoid pain, but when it does arrive, we can accept its presence and seek to release whatever it holds.

When we are in agony, we are in so much pain it is intolerable. Agony can come in the form of spiritual, emotional and also physical pain. Agony is a term we used to describe a pain that is felt so deeply that we feel we cannot overcome it, nor can we ignore it or set it free.

Agony is a wave that rises up over us and crashes down on our heart, our mind, and our body. Without agony, we are in homeostasis and we are free. When we are in agony, our body shuts down to protect us as the only thing it can focus on are the levels of pain and when they will end.

If you are in agony, we ask that you seek out the help you need. If you are in pain, we ask that you deal with it before it turns into agony. Agony, when it escalates, puts us in a position of limited control. However, pain, when it is still pain, is manageable. There are however some days and times where we are in agony and we cannot control it, nor can we fight it before it arrives.

If an event occurs and brings agony into your heart, mind or soul, accept it as it not going anywhere. Once agony has arrived, it must run its course before it leaves. There are times when agony comes in the form of sadness, anger or pain at the loss of something or someone in our lives. When these feelings arise, sit with them and learn from them. Accept how you feel as it is only through acceptance that relief and healing will eventually come.

If the pain is physical, then we must seek the attention or aid of people who can help shift this pain as agony in the body is a sure sign that something has gone wrong. However, sometimes agony takes over the body in its entirety and we must sit with it until the pain passes. Life does not always hold the answers or reasoning we seek and agony is part of our existence, as is happiness, joy and feeling spritely in our steps towards a new life.

Accept that we will experience all manners of emotions and pain during our lifetime and nothing will surprise you. It is not a case of being ready for such pain and waiting for it to arrive. It is a case of knowing that pain exists in the world, in the people around us and being tender to that. For when we are in agony, others will come to our aid, just as we should come to theirs when we sense the same.

It is through sharing our love with the world and with our fellow plants, people and animals that we will cast our pain into the light until it arrives again. We cannot avoid pain, but when it does arrive, we can accept its presence and seek to release whatever it holds. However, if pain has already escalated to agony, which it so often does, once again accept that it is there, ask how long it will stay and what you can do to make its stay shorter.

116

SYMBOLS

When we see a symbol, we will know in our heart what it means. What we must learn is that some symbols are far more subtle than others.

On the path to enlightenment, there are particular symbols we are looking for to show us that we are on the right track. Sometimes these symbols can come in the form of numbers, energy or even as physical manifestations that appear in front of us.

The symbols we encounter and the meaning behind them help us to know and find our way on the path. They help us understand if we are on track or if we have ways and means to go.

When we see a symbol, we will know in our heart what it means. What we must learn is that some symbols are far more subtle than others. What we must establish is whether the symbol is encouraging us to go further in the direction we are asking to go in or to turn around and make another way forward.

Symbols can cover both life and death, birth and rebirth, prosperity and pain, hope and joy and love and laughter.

Life and the elements within us are always communicating with us and it is through their communication, consciously and unconsciously that we will grow. It is through understanding how the Earth is communicating with us that we will see a new future arrive at our door. If we can learn to read the signs of the sky, the Earth, the water and fire we can know which elements are speaking with us and what purpose they have.

If we can understand the meaning of animals and why they have appeared at our feet or in the skies above us, we can know what they are trying to tell us merely by their presence.

If we can learn to read the weather and what the clouds are showing us in their formations, we can learn to add another language of the Earth to our repertoire which will help us make our way through our time here.

All of the Earth and its plants, people, animals, and elements are always wishing to communicate with us. It is just that we do not listen and we do not learn.

If we can learn to take in and be aware of what nature is trying to tell us, we can deepen our experience here and shorten the journey we are traveling. Just like signs tell us when there is a dead-end approaching, so can the Eagle tell you when you have lost your way or how to find a new way.

Just as weather temperature apps can tell you when bad weather is approaching, so can the sky tell you when prosperity is coming or when you should hold on making important decisions. The languages of the Earth are many, but there are many ways for you to learn and the benefits you will experience from these relationships will successfully see you through for all of your days.

It is through learning the ways of others that we may find ourselves. It is by learning the languages of others that we can successfully make our way through a new country, place or territory.

Knowing nature is knowing ourselves, and many people around the world can help you learn these skills. If you wish to navigate the path to enlightenment with a compass or not based on intuition alone, then learn what nature and the Earth are trying to tell you. This will make your journey faster and allow you to travel with more ease.

117

ARRIVAL

The path offers us nothing and everything in a single breath and it is travelling without expectations that brings us the greatest joy.

You will know you have arrived at a major checkpoint on your journey when every molecule in your body says yes to the place you have reached, however, see this place as only temporary as the path to enlightenment never ends. It is cyclical as this is the nature of life on Earth and also in the sky. It is for this reason we speak to you of enjoying the journey and not taking the journey because of the destination.

Because we cannot guarantee the destination will ever be reached, many travelers will turn back or walk away at this point. This is something we anticipate, and when the time is right, we know they will return.

However, for those who wish to invest their life and lives in this trek into the wilderness of your soul, then it is a worthy journey as the traveler has no other place to go or be. The development of the traveler is at their core what they are looking for. They have no more possessions to collect or experiences they wish to have more; they are committed to what the path can offer and are able to establish what is for their good and what is for their development.

When we understand that all experiences are either for our good or for our development and what we need to overcome, then all genuinely become part of the path. The experiences we have had in all of our lives on Earth make us who we are today and the path we have taken to this place is no more or less glorious than the path others have taken.

When we can appreciate the journey and know that no destinations genuinely exist, that they are merely checkpoints and achievements along the way, we are free to keep exploring forever. Unlike traditional travel where there is an itinerary and places we must see, on the path, there is nothing and everything for us to see at the same time.

In some parts of the path, there is darkness for weeks at a time. On other parts of the path, there is only brilliant sunshine that is almost so intolerable we need to close our eyes. The path offers us nothing and everything in a single breath and it is traveling without expectations that brings us the greatest joy.

There is a certain freedom and joy that comes with not knowing if we will ever arrive and it takes the pressure off needing to go so fast. Of course, for those who travel with no barriers in their way, the journey will be more comfortable. For those who can throw away any preconceived ideas of how much joy they will experience, it is these people who will experience the most joy as it will be unexpected. For those who invest in the path and wish to see returns for their efforts, their pockets will remain empty and the journey will feel longer than expected even though the distance remains the same.

The path does not promise to fulfill us as it is up to us to do that for ourselves. Train yourself to travel without expectation of yourself and others. Train yourself to look for the joy in even the smallest moments and use every second as an opportunity to learn about yourself and the world around you and your travels will be happy and free.

Expect the path to give you the world and all that you are looking for and it won't. The path does not make any promises, nor does it offer itself to you unless you offer yourself to it, without expectation, without the promise of a reward and without the guarantee of ever arriving. It is through traveling as spirit that we will have the true experience of life on Earth.

118

RESISTANCE

The mind is a powerful instrument that can create healing within the body. Where the body can sometimes not be perceived to survive on its own, the mind can encourage healing that the body would not otherwise engage in or with.

Resistance in the mind and body is what causes us to stray from our heart's desires.

Often the heart has a way in which it would like to go, but the motivations of the mind are different from that of the heart, and the mind provides a blockage that prevents the heart from passing through. This is something we must work to overcome as it is not necessary and the mind should not control the heart.

The mind and heart should instead be in conversation, not that one controls or defines the action of another. Where this is different is with the mind and the body.

The mind is a powerful instrument that can create healing within the body. Where the body can sometimes not be perceived to survive on its own, the mind can encourage healing that the body would not otherwise engage in or with.

If the mind can learn the infinite potential that lies within it to help the body heal, the body has a worthy ally and protector who can help it heal from almost any ailment or affliction. If the mind is not strong, however, the body as dense as it is will simply try to restore itself to its homeostasis, which is often not possible on its own. What the mind can do that the body cannot is overcome obstacles within it. Where the body sees weakness or disease within itself, the mind can change these perceived parameters and overcome them.

For example, a muscle in the body that is weak will remain weak unless it is physically worked on. However, if the mind helps the body understand that the muscle can be developed with no exercise, only mind control, then the mind itself can strengthen the muscle. We are not saying it is not important to exercise; we are exploring the potential that the mind has to strengthen the physical body we reside in so that it may last longer and help us achieve our overall goals and life purpose. It would be a shame if the physical body did not last, and yet the mind could have helped the situation.

There are cases though where the mind itself can slow down the body and create disease and ill health. This is when the mind is not working for the body; it is working against it. If we can learn to recognize what our body is doing and whether our mind is working for or against our body, we can then learn to retrain the mind to be even more efficient or to change its perspective and focus onto healing.

This is an important skill for us to learn and something we will explore further in time. For the time being, think about the health of your body and whether it could be better than it is now. Now question if your mind is working to help this situation or to hinder it. If your mind is trying to help but is doing so unsuccessfully, what can you do to change this situation? If the mind is working against the body, how can you seek to reprogram it visually and mentally to change how the mind sees the body and the potential that lies within it?

It is only through knowing the relationship between the mind and the body that we can seek to alter the relationship for our benefit.

119

FREEDOM

Time spent on this path of accumulation and paying debts is time not spent on your life purpose, which is the whole reason you exist.

Freedom is what we seek here on Earth, yet until we realize that the nature of life on Earth is slavery, we will never be free.

What is perplexing to us as beings of the sky is that human beings on Earth create their own chains and lock themselves into them, sometimes for days and sometimes for lifetimes. What we ask you to realize is we did not create these chains, you did it yourselves.

Where we work with you to train your mind, heart, and spirit to be free, you will yourself to be locked down and to chains that were never intended to exist. Where we wish for you to experience the wide-open spaces of many countries and places, you tie yourself to one place and one territory, letting yourself roam free a few weeks of the year.

Human beings were never intended to be so steadfast to the ground. We always wished that you would travel and see the world as this is part of your development. We understand you can argue that money is required to partake in these journeys, but what we ask you to reassess is how much your need for money is focussed on acquiring things to pad out your journey.

How much money is spent on building a castle around you, towers of concrete that hold your kingdom safe and sound, separated from others within the community?

How much money is spent on the nice clothing you wear and what you cover your children and pets in?

How much money is spent on living a life of luxury or keeping up with the people around you, when you could live a more minimal life and enjoy a lifetime of experiences that will broaden both your mind and your heart?

These are all questions we wish you to ask of yourself. These are all questions that are important for your growth. For you to understand what you are missing, you must first see what you are miss-spending your money and your time on.

Most of you spend your time on Earth slaving to a job that you do not enjoy or wish to pursue. This time is spent away from your family and friends, all so that you may keep up with a society that has no interest in your development or your stability. The wheel of society only wishes for more momentum and growth, and when you are thrown off this wheel, the people running it will not jump off to save you. They will just find another human to take your place.

Life will not define itself for you, but what you must know is that you can define it and how humans live now was not the way we wished for you. We wished for you to live a life of freedom and to enjoy the experiences, sights, and sounds that Earth creates. Yet you lock yourselves in offices accepting that you must pay your dues to society.

No man, woman or child owes society anything, not least your time or your energy. All you must do while you are here is focus on the ones you love and yourself. Care for the Earth, her plants, animals, and people, but do not sign yourself up for a life of slavery as we never asked for this.

Time spent on this path of accumulation and paying debts is time not spent on your life purpose, which is the whole reason you exist. To pursue your life purpose and to help others pursue theirs is why you are here. Do not mistake the demands of society for ones that you should or need to comply with. No man, woman or child should live in slavery and in this book we are trying to free your mind from these shackles. Remember this as you define your future path. All we wish is for your success and freedom from pain and suffering.

We ask that you look for joy in the smallest moments and look to others who have freed themselves from these chains. There are ways of making money that do not sacrifice your soul or your time here.

Time is all you have, and it can be taken away from you in a second. Ponder for a moment that in this second life exists and in the next, it may be gone. Know that while life is guaranteed right now as you breathe, that in the next moment life can be as far away from you than you could ever comprehend.

Do not spend your time working for a system that does not exist and does not care for your welfare. Care for your life, the lives and of others and the Earth from which you gain life from. If you can do this, you will find happiness, purpose and fulfill your soul's mission.

TRAFFIC

Life presents us with thousands of roads we could take and one very limited fuel tank.

Time spent in traffic is time wasted. Except, traffic does not only happen on the streets but also in our heart's and minds when we have too many commitments.

When we allow ourselves to be stuck in traffic, we waste time. The valuable time we have is spent navigating issues and problems that hold no relevance for us. We are merely stuck in them because we took to the road at the wrong time.

Time spent in traffic is time we will never get back, therefore, when you are thinking about getting involved in something, think about the time and toll it will take on you.

Think about the potential time you could be spending on what matters to you. Too often, human beings spend time on everything that does not matter, leaving very minimal time to work on what does. This is a shame as what matters to us should be taking up all of our time.

When we become stuck in traffic in the ways and lives of others and their actions, our mind and heart become congested. To remove this congestion uses the very little fuel we have to navigate out of situations that did not require us to be there in the first place.

If you are smart, you will always have a full fuel tank and only take trips that you are going to enjoy. Getting involved in the mischief and mania of others uses fuel that you cannot afford to reproduce. Instead, spend your time and your energy on journeys that further your development and do not hinder them. Spend your time planning where you wish to go and on the most effective routes of getting there with minimal traffic. Find places on the way where you can restore your energy and refuel. This may come in the form of spending time with loved ones or something as simple as meditation.

Life presents us with thousands of roads we could

take and one very limited fuel tank. Remember this as you offer to drive people to places that do not matter to you. Remember this when your fuel is getting low and you don't have enough to get to your actual destination, the one you are trying to reach. Think how many wasted days you have accumulated getting involved in topics or experiences that are not yours to own or partake in.

In life, we have many choices. Who, what and where you spend your time are some of the most important choices you will ever make. Make them wisely and you will reach the destination you seek. Take journeys down roads you have not planned for that are defined by people or motivations you do not care about and the time you have to reach your destination will be slim.

There are of course beautiful diversions with the people we love, but all roads should lead back to home and to our original place of birth. Our birth rite and our soul's purpose. Living to aid the life purposes of others and neglecting our own may be selfless, but it accomplishes nothing when the true purpose of our time here is to find our own soul's purpose and fulfill that. Who, what and where we spend our time in between is up to us.

COURTNEY BECK

The journey is as long or as windy as you make it. Remember this.

121

THE WILL TO LIVE

Life was born to be lived, not taken, by you, me or any other life-force on Earth. The only way death comes to you is by death itself.

When we have a will to live, we strive to do all that is possible to retain our life here. What is unfortunate is that when the body becomes old, sick or tired, that fight becomes harder to win. Not that it is about winning or losing as life is always lost in the end, but often we have more work to do before our departure, but we allow our bodies to give up before that time arrives.

The true and ideal time of death is when all of our work has been done, and we are satisfied with the impact we have left and are ready to move to the next plane.

What is unfortunate is sometimes that time arrives before we expect or need it to. This can come in the form of others using their free will to our detriment, natural disasters, car accidents and other senseless ends that are out of our control. What we cannot control is how we will meet our end. What we can control is what we do with our time up until that point.

If you are wise, you will work to realize your true purpose. If you are strong, you will fight for your body to remain here, against all the odds and in all environments and situations. The mind is stronger than the body, but sometimes the body chooses to leave this plane as it does not believe it can keep up the fight. Life on Earth is truly a choice and one that we can end at any point in time. We can choose life as life chooses us, or we can end life and choose to move to the next world.

What we must clarify here is what happens when a person takes their own life, as there is a difference between the body fighting to live out of sickness, accidents or disease and choosing to leave versus the act of taking our own life by our own hand.

Where we understand the act of moving to the other side when the mind and body does not perceive they can carry on, on the other side we will show you how you could plan for next time. When you arrive here, the physical body is with you no longer and remains as a shell on Earth. Everything here is healed and you have all the answers you did not otherwise have in real life. What you have given up is your life purpose, your family, friends, life, and experiences on Earth. For those hanging by a thread, we understand this decision to carry on to this place as the journey on Earth when the body is so physically impacted is much harder. This we understand.

What we do not understand is when a human being wishes to take to their own life and does so on the Earthly plane. We recognize this is your choice, as we recognize all the other choices you can make. However, this choice comes with consequences and ones you may not necessarily understand.

When the life you live is taken by your own hand, that is an act against yourself. The taking of your own life is not noble, and it is not the best idea you will ever have. The best idea you will ever have when in this situation is to stay, fight and know that death will come for you when the time is right. At this time, it is not when you should commit an act of violence against yourself, no matter how gentle you perceive it to be.

Whether it is by medicine, a rope or by drowning, no way is gentle when the soul is in terror. What you must understand is the body does not understand, condone or ask for acts of violence against itself. Just as on Earth we do not condone acts of violence against another human being. It is for this reason that the soul of someone who has committed suicide must be dealt with gently, but also with a firm hand as the rest they are looking for will not come in this plane. Those who commit suicide must realize the consequences of their actions and see the impact it has had on Earth, to their family, friends and those who loved them. Even their pets.

What we wish to turn around is that this decision does not happen in another life, as some people continue this pattern many times over. It is like the suicide itself leaves an imprint and a pathway that makes it seem like an option the next time around also. We are not presenting you with this option in the next life. What the next life presents is a test that asks you not to take this path even though you know it is available to you.

It is when this situation arises again that we wish for you to connect back with your soul, in this moment of pain and know that it is not the right decision. It is a decision that will put you back many lifetimes. It is a decision that hurts those around you when the hurt you feel can be subsided even in your moments of darkness.

Life is a gift and although we understand it does not always feel this way, what you must understand is that the taking of a life has extensive karmic consequences, just as the taking of one's own life has these consequences too. Where repeating lives can be avoided is that when this decision comes around again, declining this path and moving to the light can erase all that has been done before.

If you know someone who has taken their own life, know that we are caring for them as best as we can and are talking them through the decisions they have made and are working with them to heal. Know that in the next life they will be presented with this choice again and we make both paths available, not to be cruel or unkind, but to give human beings the opportunity to choose life over death and to know that they are not their own god. Death comes for us when we least expect it, and it is not our job to take someone else's life or to take our own, just as we will not come for you any earlier than what has already been defined. We cannot control the actions of others or their ill intent, but for those who have taken the life of another, their actions will be dealt with accordingly here on the other side and in further lives to come.

Life was born to be lived, not taken, by you, me or any other life-force on Earth. The only way death comes to you is by death itself.

Sometimes we are faced with choices when we are placed in situations where our body is diseased or significant impact has been made to the body. When and if these decisions come your way, what you must decide is if you are willing to continue despite the consequences. We cannot give you a new body, but you can experience life in a new way and still fulfill your purpose.

We are always here to help you live, and even in death we will help you there, but death by your own hand is something we must work with. Much like repeating a year at school, life repeats again for those who are lost and need a new opportunity to find their way. We work with all of those who have lost their way on finding it again. We give you this knowledge so that you may know that while your life is your choice, the impact it has can have lifetimes of influence, for better or for worse.

122

SACRIFICE

No man ever climbed to the top of a mountain following the safest route and no woman ever sailed around the world knowing that it was going to be smooth sailing.

When we sacrifice ourselves, our livelihood and our security for our life purpose, we are pursuing it wholeheartedly, and with such faith, it will shake the heavens.

When human beings arrive on Earth, we give you a life purpose to fulfill. Not because we like handing out tasks, but because the Earth, its people, plants, and animals need saving and we ask for your help in doing this. A life purpose can be heavy, light, sad or happy, depending on the role you have been given.

Perhaps your role in this life is to work with animals,

nature, to help human beings pass from this life to the next or to write books that help save humanity. All roles are important, even if to you they seem insignificant as each life and impact has a domino effect. While you may perceive yourself to be a simple cafe worker, the smile you give to someone else can be the difference between life or death depending on how they feel that day and the decisions they are contemplating making.

For the man who collects garbage, he is helping clean the Earth and fight waste, and for the woman who spends her days nursing an elderly parent, she is helping him or her pass successfully, faithfully and with love from this life to the next. All of us have a heart and love to share, how we show it through our daily actions and impact is what makes our lives here complete.

If you are unsure what your life purpose is, now is the time to find out. If you have questions about your past lives and the actions you took within them, there are people, healers who can access these lives and help you release the pain or trauma accumulated within them. If you face a difficult decision about who to help on what day, do the best you can and you will still be rewarded.

When those around you are working on their life purpose and they commit wholeheartedly to it, celebrate them for this. It is not easy to leave your livelihood for one that is unknown or to sacrifice the safety of the life you live to do something that is completely unknown or out of favor with society.

Those who pursue their life purpose and sacrifice what they have to do so are brave and should be commended for their efforts. It is easy to live an easy life on Earth and to face the daily mundane challenges we do. It is far harder to throw our lives and our identity on the line for something we do not know or trust, that has not been proven to us yet.

It is easy to take the path well-trodden and to follow others' footsteps. It is far harder to carve out and pave your own path so that others may know they can do the same.

Life on Earth provides us with an opportunity to sacrifice what we do not need daily. Whether we cling to what we have or let it go for an unknown higher good is up to us. The more you are willing to give, the higher the rewards, but there are also higher risks. No man ever climbed to the top of a mountain following the safest route and no woman ever sailed around the world knowing that it was going to be smooth sailing.

When you are trying to achieve your purpose, there are risks of rain, hail and also the wildest storms of your existence. What you must understand is that whatever you spend your time doing, you are at risk of all of the above anyway. Isn't it better to chase your dreams and ride the wildest of waves than to spend your life waiting for the rain to come doing something that does not express your heart or your mind?

All are decisions you are faced with here on Earth. The waves will come for you anyway. Be brave and choose the boat that is not the safest, but the one that will take you the fastest way to your destination. You could take a ship and have a safe and slow ride here on Earth, or you could grab a small sailing boat, sail off into the wind and pursue a life worth living and worthy of you and all of the lives you have had to lead to arrive at this place. The choice is yours.

May the wind always be at your back and may your hands remain like steel at the wheel of your life. It is the mind of the sailor that takes them through the storm. Even the biggest ships can sink and often it is the tiniest boats on the wildest adventures that pop up after the storm, untouched, unscathed and ready to take on the next leg of their mission.

NATURE

It is not your right to take a life, for food or otherwise. If a life is taken, the consequences of these actions must be taken on board.

When we are in nature, we can be free. Free to connect to the grass, the sky, trees, flowers, plants and animals. When we are in cities, we are trapped by concrete and nature has been choked out of the city due to high rise buildings and pollution.

There is a reason those who live in the country are healthier and it is because the air is purer. There is a reason that people in the country are happier and it is because they remain connected to nature in a way that is not tangible, but it leaves a beautiful imprint on their soul.

When we breathe the same air as the trees, we are

renewed. When we can take in nature, the beauty of it and what it can offer us apart from its love, we realize that in the scheme of the universe we are one small piece of a web that is made up of billions of other pieces. What we must realize is that all pieces are equal and should, therefore, be treated equally. It is not your right to take a life, for food or otherwise. If a life is taken, the consequences of these actions must be taken on board.

To vibrate at our highest levels, a plant-based diet suits us all most, but some will never adhere to or listen to what their vibration needs or asks for.

When you look to the heavens, what do you see? Do you see a monkey climbing a tree or a phoenix on fire in the sky? What the clouds show us is also part of nature and we must not mistake greenery or animals as being the only parts of nature as nature exists in all parts of our world, even the layers of atmosphere that protect us. In time you will understand this more. In time you will understand that to be free, you must free all others from their slavery and oppression.

You may free people, plants, and animals from their imaginary masters, from their masters in the real world and from the elements that drain and empty them of life and love.

When you see those around you in slavery, whether they have done it to themselves or have been enslaved through unfortunate circumstances, do what you can to make their life and their way easier. If you can cut them from their chains, do this. If you cannot, but you can ease the wounds they carry, do this.

Where we may be enslaved to a society that does not work to our highest good, we can always be free in our minds if we wish to be.

124

CUSTODIANS

When we are custodians, we have had trust placed in us that we will do the right thing, at all times and in all weathers.

To be a custodian is to be a guardian, of land, of people, of space, plants or animals.

When we are custodians, we have had trust placed in us that we will do the right thing, at all times and in all weathers.

There is a difference between a traditional custodian though and ownership. Where a custodian works with the land, its people, plants or animals, appreciating the needs of all within a space, there is collaboration and appreciation. The custodian has love for the space and works to preserve and grow new life within the space and look after the life of all that resides there too.

All of this work comes from love, and it does not feel like work because it is love. We know when we are in love or love somebody because we serve them without prejudice, judgement and a need to receive something in return.

When we own something in society, we seek to protect it, but not for the right reasons. We seek to protect it because it is a commercial asset and one that makes us money. We seek to protect it because it is 'ours'. Nothing on this Earth is ours and it never has been. Every creature on this Earth was born from the womb of the universe and the universe is its mother.

What we believe we own is a piece of paper in a society that could fall over tomorrow. What we believe we own is a piece of time and space in a universe that is always changing. It is perceived ownership and this is where custodianship is different. Where a custodian may look after a certain territory, they do not presume to own it, they help advance it. Not for monetary gain, but because they wish to look after who and what is there. To look after the space and the Earth that feeds these creatures is important also. Remember this.

When walking through the world, aim to meet other custodians and learn from them. Learn how they see the world and their place within it. It is from this that you can form a new worldview and new ways of working to save the greenery we live and work on. We cannot pillage the Earth and expect it to remain the same way forever. We cannot preserve tiny spaces to remind us of what life on Earth did look like. The entire Earth must be preserved and we must stop this senseless self-development now. The Earth has become a mine and one that will eventually run out.

What will you do when all of the spaces have run out? What will you do when there is nothing left to eat or to drink? What will you dream of then?

You will dream of what the world was like before you destroyed it. This is what will consume you and it is only through this longing and this pain that you will be able to start again.

125

CHRISTMAS

Christmas is a time to celebrate the year, but it is also a powerful week to contemplate the difference you wish to make in the world next year.

When Christmas comes, another year is gone. Another year of wasting and wanting, needing and consuming, experiencing and creating, loving and losing.

In our lives and our times, there is a constant cycle of life and death, beginnings and endings. When you realize this, you will know that with each ending there is another beginning and with each beginning, there is sure to be another end.

When the years go by, without rhyme or reason, we can often question where all of our time went. Christmas is a time to celebrate the year, but it is also a powerful week to contemplate the difference you wish to make in the world next year. You can do this at any time of course, but if you are smart, you will use Christmas as your gauge and clock for how much time has passed and what you have or have not done.

While Christmas has become about spending time with the ones you love, giving and receiving gifts, we urge you to think about what gifts you will give the Earth? What of your gifts will you give the Earth?

We are each born with gifts and these gifts are important for us to use. Otherwise, they will expire. Like a jar of something you keep in the fridge, you can keep it forever, but the contents may fade and lose their life. It the same with your body and mind as it gets older. The heart is the only thing that stays young if we let it. When you can realize that what lies within your body are gifts you can share and were born to share, you can use them before your body expires. To leave them in wait is to leave a beautiful jam, sitting in its jar, never tasted and never consumed.

In the context of your life, you have so much to give, yet so often you spend your time on things, people and problems that do not matter. Leave these things, open the jar and see what is inside. You have nothing left to lose and everything to gain from using these gifts that are your birth rite. To not use them is to let them go. To not use them is to disregard the magic that is inside you. To embrace them is to feel and see a power that is unstoppable, a force that is as strong as life itself.

Use your gifts, seek to find out what they are and use them to transform yourself and the world around you. Gifts aren't given to not be used. They are to be used fully, intentionally and until the jar is empty, life is over and it begins again.

At Christmas time, see the gifts you have been given, but wonder about the gifts you have not yet opened. On your birthday, see the gifts your loved ones have brought you, but know the most important gifts were given to you at your birth. This is what you must remember and discover within yourself. We love you.

126

ELASTICITY

When we try to restrict the growth of our dreams and wishes to fit a certain shape, we miss out on the shape they could grow into if they were allowed to grow naturally and without restriction.

When you are chasing the dreams you have created in your mind; you cannot be rigid in their release, you must be like elastic. Dreams come to us in a way that cannot be controlled as they are a heartfelt response to something our soul wishes to achieve.

For some people, this may be writing a book, poetry, a song or creating the tallest building in the world. All of us have dreams and wishes, and this is a natural part of being a human being. The nature of being here is that we wish to create and transform our dreams and wishes from seeds into great trees, humble and strong.

When we try to restrict the growth of our dreams and wishes to fit a certain shape, we miss out on the shape they could grow into if they were allowed to grow naturally and without restriction. Like in life, we cannot control which shape we grow into or how tall we are. For a dream to truly take shape, we must let it grow like all of Earth's other elements grow. We must allow it to take shape in the way it wishes to, as a dream is merely the seed of a thought that is passing through the universe waiting for someone to reach out and grab it.

Some of our dreams are linked to our life purpose and some are not. Some people dream of going to Mexico or Egypt and others dream of stopping starvation in a world where so many starve and others over-consume. The nature of a person's dream is not up to us to judge. It is whether they can accomplish this dream that we support them in. When a dream is born, it is created as an 'I wonder' and in time it turns to an 'I wish'. It is over time and with energy that it turns into an 'I can' and from there, if courage and heart are poured into it the dream begins to take form.

If we have a dream we wish to take shape, we must allow it to grow and not to constrict it from fear of it not turning out. If we are connecting with the universe and wishing the best, helping it form and be nurtured, we will see its growth. What we are trying to say is that if you allow a dream to grow naturally, with elasticity and without rigidity, it can grow into something far greater as it will be powered by the universe.

Hold onto your dreams, but also be prepared to let go of them to the point where they are a helium balloon, tied to your wrist on a string. The balloon is likely to go further the longer you let the string out and when it is in flight, the wind can carry it too. The energy you put into it is the helium and your real-world actions are the string. This is one way you can support a dream by letting it grow and fly without total control.

Or you can hold the helium balloon close to your chest and never let it take flight because it could pop. What you must know is that it could pop in your arms purely because of the weight you are putting on it. Let the balloon go and you will see it fly. Hold it too close and you will see it pop.

The restrictions we put on our dreams or the rigidity

we pursue them with can be the hole that lets the air out of the balloon we are so desperately trying to preserve. The greatest lesson we can learn when it comes to our hopes and dreams is to create what we wish for and to do as much as we can to ensure a perfect launch and then let the balloon go, without attachment to the outcome and without stress.

To let go is to see a dream go far wider and beyond anything you could ever have hoped or dreamed of. It is when we let go of our dreams and ask the universe to take hold of and support them that the world becomes a truly magical place.

If you have a dream you are hoping to pursue, do not be like a string, rigid and controlling, be like elastic and know when the time is right, you'll throw it away and let your balloon take flight.

127

CELEBRATION

In time, what you will come to realise is that even when we lose, we are still winning as a loss still represents a gain if we take the time to look at it and learn from it.

In this Earth and at this time we do not celebrate enough.

Instead of cherishing the small wins we have and even the large ones, we often keep moving to the next task or job. Some would say this is an affliction gained by a society too focussed on success. I would say it is caused by a lack of self-love and a constant need to prove one's worth in a society that does not value it.

When we come to Earth, we celebrate the journey ahead and our arrival. Time on Earth is something that is known for the physical, mental and emotional rigor required to make it through. Earth is one of the harsher planets to spend time on because of the species that live on it. I am not talking about animals, I speak of people.

People are a tough species to navigate and negotiate with because primarily we are self-serving, but we are also not self-loving. We come to Earth pure of heart only to lose our purity when we become focussed on proving ourselves and our worth. If over time, we can learn that we will never be good enough for the limitations and checkpoints that society has created, we can then begin traveling our own journey which is what this book is about.

If you know you will never satisfy the gods of Earth and those who perceive themselves to be this way; then you can begin with learning how to satisfy yourself and the wishes of what your soul wants to accomplish. If we can help you learn what your soul needs, you then have the toolkit you need to begin accomplishing the life you wished for on Earth.

Over the course of our life, we will experience many highs and lows, wins and losses, but what we must remember is to celebrate the wins.

Wins are so fleeting here on Earth, and if we do not celebrate these for what they are, we will begin to grow tired of our time here. When we celebrate where we have won and accomplished something, this provides us time to sit with the win, realize how far we have come and where we wish to go next. A society built on speed never wholly manages to make good decisions as good decisions take time. It is, of course, great to have momentum and we encourage this, but not to the detriment of your journey or to meet the needs of others.

If you can learn to let your soul take flight, you will experience many wins, and you will go higher than any star or planet you have ever seen.

If you spend your life too grounded, always moving from one task to the next, one win to the next loss, you will never experience the joy of what you are trying to create. In time, what you will come to realize is that even when we lose, we are still winning as a loss still represents a gain if we take the time to look at it and learn from it. It is the gap in time between a win and a loss or a loss and a win where we make our best decisions. It is through realizing that every loss is a win as it can be learned from that we will realize our full potential.

Cherish the wins, but also cherish the losses as both are an opportunity to learn, an opportunity to celebrate the road we have traveled to reach this point and space to plan what's next. The space between a decision is as valuable as the decision itself.

128

VISION

If you can sell what you love and what you wish to gift to the world, at least you can fill your heart and your pockets at the same time.

When we have a vision, we have a picture we are attempting to paint.

When we have a painting, this is something we can sell. If we can learn to paint, we can sell our paintings forever. If we only ever dream of painting, we will only ever see paintings in our mind.

Selling our wares on Earth is something that will sustain us both physically and emotionally. Selling the wares of another will never have the same level of satisfaction. If we can learn to sell the skills we have, we can have a life of love, pain, and enjoyment.

You may wonder why I said pain and it is because pain is part of everything as pain is often the catalyst for creation. It is through lack that we know what to create and what we need more of. It is through joy that we can see where there was lack and why something's birth or creation is so important.

If you have a vision for what you would like to bring to the world, you must set about creating it. The path to enlightenment is one that will take you forever and a day to complete. Over that time you must still survive and support yourself in a world focused on paper money. If you can sell what you love and what you wish to gift to the world, at least you can fill your heart and your pockets at the same time.

If you live a life of fear, never knowing what you should create and if it would be good enough, then you will miss out on all of the joy and only ever have a pocket and heart that is half full. What we wish for you to do is discover your gifts so that you can live the great life you had always planned to. Following your purpose does not mean leading a poor life, it means living a rich life of sacrifice.

To bring a dream to fruition, there will always be sacrifices. Just as to create a cake you will first need to buy your ingredients and learn how to cook. The life purpose we have is an innate talent and gift, but it will need to be worked on and invested in. If you can pour your heart and your soul into this endeavor and not measure yourself on money, fame, stardom or the love of others, you will do fine. Fine is the minimum you will do. If you can pour your heart and soul into learning what you need to, your dreams can be filled with light, color and be born into a reality where money is paid for what you produce.

We cannot change the society you were born into, but we can help you adapt to and journey through it in the healthiest way possible. We love you and support your vision if you have one you wish to create. Even if you do not, we have answers for you that could help you find your way to your north star.

Carrying money without love will never bring you what you are looking for. Carrying your wares with a pocket full of gold and happiness in your heart is a dream you can have for a society that is still learning what it should value. Money is the gesture you can offer someone who is trying to create. Love is what you are given in return.

We will love you always, no matter what you do or

create as we see you for your soul, not for how heavy your pockets are.

129

MENTAL STRESS

When stress bends our minds, forcing us to find different solutions to old problems in a new and rejuvenated way, then what was stress can give us innovation.

When we are mentally stressed, it can break us, but it can also force us to grow.

In the lives we lead here on Earth, there are all matters and kinds of stress. Even deciding what to eat for lunch can be stressful, but it need not be. What humans have forgotten how to do is to think for themselves and to decide what is worth being stressed about and what is not. There is a difference.

Life, our attachment to it and the ending of it is something that can induce stress which is natural because we only know life and do not know death.

However, we cannot control when we die, therefore there is no point in wasting time and energy on something so unknown to us that will be over in a second. Death and dying are the single biggest stress to all of us, yet we spend our days and nights worrying about small mundane things like when the internet is not working or what our colleague may be saying behind our back.

In ancient times there was disease, in prehistoric times there were extreme conditions and giant predators who could take our lives in a heartbeat. This was stressful, but it needed to be because we needed to mentally stretch our brains to solve these problems.

When stress breaks us for unnecessary and unequivocally simple things, we have wasted our lives on what does not matter never allowing us to tackle or fight for what does. When stress bends our minds, forcing us to find different solutions to old problems in a new and rejuvenated way, then what was stress can give us innovation.

There is a reason why people who don't give up do better during their time here, and it is because they persist beyond the point that other people will. Where other people throw in the reigns or give up the fight, these people figure out what they need to do to ride the horse in a way where they do not need reigns. When they are in the ring, they put down their gloves and fight bare-knuckled. These are the signs of a true fighter and someone who is willing to give their all for the greater good and for their greater good. Without these people, nothing would ever get done.

If you are under stress, sort out in your mind what matters versus what doesn't. To make it easier for you, what matters is your life, but worrying about when you will die is pointless because you do not control this. What matters is you achieving your life purpose and the reason you have come to Earth in the first place. Worrying about your colleagues and what to have for lunch should not induce stress, it should produce a response worthy of the level it presents.

If you cannot decide what to eat for lunch, try somewhere new. If your colleagues are giving you a hard time, find a new job. Life presents us with so many options this is stressful in itself, but it need not be. With the right attitude, you can learn to bend rather than break and what you will find is that it is in the bend that your greatest work and self will shine through.

If we do not bend to our environment, we will never grow. Just as if we break, we will lose our chance of doing something incredible here on Earth in the limited amount of time we have here. It is your choice of how rigid or flexible you will be with this. Make your decision now.

130

COMA

Some people will live in a comatose state for their entire existence here, never realising the full potential they could accomplish if they were willing to take a risk and brave enough to open their eyes to what is really happening here on Earth.

When we are in a coma, we are asleep and in a state of unconscious. This is what can also happen to people though when they are awake. The world is in a coma, and we must all wake up. We must wake up to ourselves, each other and the damage we are doing to the world we inhabit and consume.

Those who are in a coma appear to be asleep. They follow their daily routine like there is no thought involved. They move from one task to the next, effortlessly, but with no speed or grace. They are like robots completing chores, never asking when the day will begin or when it will end. If we are wise, we will wake up to the fact that the world is asleep and needs waking up. Without more people awake, the coma we are in will slowly but surely destroy everything we cherish and need to live here in a wholly happy way.

Some people will live in a comatose state for their entire existence here, never realizing the full potential they could accomplish if they were willing to take a risk and brave enough to open their eyes to what is really happening here on Earth. These people may never wake up.

Others who are in a semi-conscious state may see snippets of what has gone wrong, but they will struggle with the darkness and reality of it and instead will want to shield their eyes from what's to come.

And then there are those who have their eyes open, but they are not willing to act. It is like a patient who has woken up from a coma but cannot move anything else other than their eyes and fingers. Thought is possible, but there is no room to act when they are still stuck in bed.

Finally, there are those who are awake, wholly and completely. The future of the planet lies with this group. While the rest of the world consumes all of our resources and makes no effort to put what they take back, it will be this group who will aspire to find ways to solve this situation. It will be this group who will not shield their eyes from the horrors that will follow and who will brave the storm with their eyes open, dragging everybody they can out of the rubble. It is this group who will be the peacemakers when everyone else on Earth wants to go to war.

It will not be easy for this group as they are the ones who will be ridiculed for their free-thinking, their positive attitudes and for wanting to solve problems the rest of the world does not even see as a problem. It is this group that will put their hearts and minds on the line while others will have fear in their hearts. Whether you are awake or asleep, brave enough to act or not brave enough, these are the people you must back. Without these people, we lose our potential as a planet and sacrifice it for waste and wanting more.

Take your concerns and put plans in place for how you would like to help. Take your worries and put them to work in a way that helps, not hinders the work that others are trying to do. Use your mind to spread good and your heart to spread joy and peace where there is none.

It is through joining together that we will become free again. It is through your help and what you can do in your home that will ensure the home we all live in will be more livable for others. It is through hope, kindness and bold actions that we will see the change we need here on Earth.

Will you work to help or hinder this process? Will you be brave or will you shy away from what is to come if we do not stop? Will you rise up and be the best you can be, irrespective of the consequences? Your gut feeling is giving you your answer, follow it.

GREED

If you can realise that it is by giving more that you will receive more, you will never go hungry for a day in your life. And if you do, it will help you understand what others are missing out on.

When we are greedy, we are unkind to ourselves and others. When we are greedy, we will take from the hands of others to feed ourselves. There is a difference between taking the minimum and taking everything to fill up your needs and wants.

When we have a full belly, we are not greedy. When we have an empty belly, we can be greedy. Although some people who have a full belly are still greedy and those with an empty belly are not. How do we explain this?

When the mind and heart are full, the belly can be

empty, but you can still feel full. When the mind and heart are empty, it is easy to feel like you want to fill yourself with more as there is a hole that cannot appear to be filled. Although some people try to keep filling it, it never works as the nature of a hole that is never-ending is that it goes on forever. What these people must realize is that when they seek to fill their hearts and minds what goes into their belly becomes less important. What they must realize is that through filling the hearts, minds, and bellies of others that we ourselves can become full, never wanting or needing anything else.

If we are smart, we will realize that when we sacrifice some of our own happiness and welfare for the welfare of others, we incur cosmic rewards meaning that good karma naturally flows to us. It is when we are naturally abundant because of our actions that we will find the satisfaction we are seeking out of life.

If you can realize the damage you do by being selfish and greedy, you can change your actions now to more positive ones. If you can realize that it is by giving more that you will receive more, you will never go hungry for a day in your life. And if you do, it will help you understand what others are missing out on.

Going without helps you to understand how lucky you are to have what you have. We cannot control the circumstances given to you, but we can control what we do within those circumstances to make others happy. Remember this when you eat your next meal, have your next snack or when you see a homeless person in the street. In the lives we live we will experience life as both the rich and the poor, and both have lessons to teach us. What you will find is that both can be generous as it is the way of the heart, not the circumstances that allow us to give back to the society we live in.

Be generous always and you will always be rewarded. Life rewards those who are kind, spirited and those who give without needing to get back. The giver in life is always the one that is the fullest in their heart, mind, and soul. The spirit does not crave food, it craves love and this we have in abundance no matter what our situation is.

DESTINY: PART 2

Reduce your footprint and maximise your impact positively and you will begin fulfilling your destiny.

The destiny we have is not set in stone, nor should it be. Destiny on Earth is a choice and a future we can either embrace or walk away from.

If we are brave, we can see the potential in ourselves or find someone who can show us the vision and the way. Once we have this vision, we can decide if we will do what we came here to do in this lifetime or the next.

If you have arrived on Earth in this lifetime, you are here to help not hinder Earth's survival. If you are reading this book, you have been given a role that you are here to fulfill and if you do not fulfill it, you are not just wasting your own potential, but Earth's potential too.

The world we live in now is not safe. Not compared to how the world was when life first began. In earlier times people were free to have ideas and were safe to express them without fear of retribution. Now we live in a time and place where ideas are squashed and squandered for other peoples' gains and losses. We live in a world where we are not cherished for having an opinion and wish to save the world; we are laughed at for thinking we could make change. Yes, as one person change is a lot harder. The point that most humans miss is what we could do and change if we all worked together and were united in our mission to change the planet and her people.

As animals and plant life die out, human beings do not see this as a warning to stop consuming; they continue to consume day in and day out always wanting more than they have right now. What we must realize is it is not about having or needing more, it is having and needing less. We have become a wasteful society born out a need to consume and fill our bellies and our pockets to the point where we need bigger bellies and pockets. This is not the way, nor has it ever been the way. Humanity has become lost and we must find ourselves again, even if that means losing all we have for the greater good of saving the Earth and everything that resides in it.

To embrace our destiny is not to try and accumulate more before we die, it is to accumulate less and make less of a footprint so that the Earth lives for longer than we do. Yes the Earth itself as a planet will not die, but what is held inside and on her can. Without trees, we cannot breathe. Without animals and plants, we will not have food. Without friendship with ourselves and each other, we do not have love and love is as important as air.

If we are brave, we will know we are here to help Earth in whatever way we can, without prejudice, without question and without the justification of how we must live. Your role here is not defined by the lifestyle you wish to lead. Your role here is defined by the output we wish you to have during your time here and the impact you will make.

Reduce your footprint and maximize your impact positively and you will begin fulfilling your destiny. To continue to waste and want is to lead a life that will not amount to anything other than that you lived a life of consumption and were part of the wheel we call life.

Be remembered for the impact you made, the love you gave and for the vision you had of a better, brighter future and you will be remembered not for the human being you wanted to be, but for the human being you were. This is what's important.

THE BODY

What we must remember is that while the body can take us up mountains, it can also throw us down the mountains we've struggled so hard to climb.

The limitations of the human body are many. Even with the strongest purpose and way of living, we can find that the body we reside in lets us down. This is the one true flaw in our existence here on Earth. Even when we look after our mind and our soul, the body's life can be cut short by diseases or even by an accident that was not part of our present or future path.

The only thing we can do with this is to work with the body, understand its flaws and know that it must be protected and enhanced as much as possible. The growth of what we have inside us does not contain only our spirit as sometimes the body can work against us. Not out of spite, but because the environment we live in or the stress we put ourselves under can pressure the body too much into submission, which allows it to fail purely based on it not receiving what it needs and staying in a state of homeostasis.

What we must remember is that while the body can take us up mountains, it can also throw us down the mountains we've struggled so hard to climb. As the adage says, 'What comes up, must come down', and this is the way of the body also. We are not able to choose when we descend, but we can choose to ascend above any challenges our body, mind or environment throws against us.

What we must ensure is that our body is strong at the bottom of the mountain before we climb it and all the way to the top. We cannot move in sprints, hoping that our body will keep the pace as pace is not something the body understands. The body cannot be reasoned with and it cannot be told 'Just a little bit longer'.

The body does not understand stress, all it feels is pain and pressure. In our lives, we underestimate how much pressure we put our mind and body under to achieve what we wish to achieve. What we do not realize is that a body and mind under pressure for too long will collapse. Like a marathon runner must rest in between races and train, they cannot run a marathon forever, just as the body cannot keep up extreme endurance for too long as it will bend and then break.

It is in the bend that we do our best work. It is when we bend for too long that we break and this is what we must all better understand. There is no strength in pushing yourself too far; there is only weakness.

True strength is in knowing when to stop, rest and begin again tomorrow or in a month's time. It is better that we spend our lives in a slow bend than to move too quickly and break. When a stick is bent, it moves back to what is nearly its original position.

When a stick snaps, there is a permanent weakness as the two halves will never make it whole again. Protect the body as a whole, protect the mind as it lies within the body and work with the heart to keep it open. The more open we are to the world around and within us, the more we know when to bend and when to avoid breaking. This is the lesson of all people on Earth.

CHILDREN

When we have children, we make a promise to fulfil our life purpose and also theirs. We offer ourselves as a gift often long before we are in a position to do so.

When we take a chance on something, we bet that it is the right move for us even with unsteady feet or an unsteady heart.

When we take a chance on something that is not real, this is the ultimate bet as it is a bet that has never been made before, nor will it be made again if it fails.

In our lives on Earth, everything we do is a bet on whether something will or won't work. When we have children, it is a bet that they will be beautiful creatures who will bring us both pain and joy. What we do not see is that it is a bet connected to our life purpose and whether we can still fulfill it with the distraction and love of another being who takes up our whole lives.

Children are the most significant gamble we make because we put our own purpose at risk by spending so much time helping them fulfill theirs.

It is when we hover over a child too much that we waste our own energy. It is when we smother a child with affection and rules that we can stunt their growth. It is when we disengage from our own lives for the benefit of our children that we risk losing ourselves and this becomes a bet we have lost.

When we have children, we make a promise to fulfill our life purpose and also theirs. We offer ourselves as a gift often long before we are in a position to do so.

When we have children too often we think about age and having children early as time-wise that is best for us when our bodies and minds are too young. What we must realize and consider is that the younger we have children, the less likely we are to fulfill our purpose. This is because when we are young we often do not know who we are ourselves. To have children too young and spend your lives on them, disregarding your own needs is to travel endlessly down a plane where you must wait for your time to begin again so that your purpose can be fulfilled.

When we are young, we are free. We bet everything we have on our survival and what we have learned so far. To win is to discover your life purpose and begin achieving it. To lose it to commit to something too early and miss the boat on what could have been smooth sailing. To lose ourselves when we have children is not a gift, it is a curse and one that we ourselves must carry.

To be selfless, we must first be selfish, and children teach us the greatest lessons about this. Remember your children, but also remember yourself as you are the light that guides their path. However, if your light goes out so can theirs, so ensure your light burns brightly always and you will have a beautiful journey here.

ANTIDOTE

If you are hurting or you have experienced trauma, know that the antidote isn't trying to suppress the trauma as this simply helps the poison of this trauma travel further into your veins.

The antidote to pain and suffering is movement. Without movement we are stuck, sinking down into the depths of our own abyss. However, with movement, we provide our body, mind, and heart with a flow that naturally sends the poison away from our heart and into the Earth again.

If you are hurting or you have experienced trauma, know that the antidote isn't trying to suppress the trauma as this simply helps the poison of this trauma travel further into your veins.

There is a reason why people who have been

poisoned only last a certain amount of time and that is because the heart continues to pump and circulate the poison for you. The heart does not know what it is doing, it just continues to function.

However, when we speak of pain and trauma, we speak of poison as something we can't change and should not suppress. We should let the poison flow through us, allowing us to experience it wholeheartedly and fully. Unlike snake medicine where we must stay still to stop the pain and poison flowing through us, when it comes to poison arrows or darts of the heart, we must continue to move so we do not stop.

Naturally, if the trauma is substantial enough, there may not be anything to keep us moving for a time or a moment. Losing someone we love is a substantial trauma and it will be hard to keep moving when the weight of pain feels so heavy we can barely even stand. However, when this time passes and you must get up for something else, use it as an opportunity to keep moving. Even if it is just a few steps, a few breaths that show you are still alive or even the vaguest heartbeat.

We must continue to feel the loss and resist the urge to switch it off. It is when pain is suppressed that we hold trauma within our body for years, generations and lifetimes to come. However, it is when we allow our pain to take us over for a time, for us to face it that it can then be released when the time is right.

The act of movement is what forces our pain to move out of our hands, feet, and breath because pain cannot stand movement and it cannot stand to be faced. Remember this the next time you are in pain and seek to move, even if it is just a finger, the dropping of a mask to show you are in pain or even a few small steps.

What is something small for someone else, like the ability to function is huge for someone who is experiencing grief. Remember this for yourself and others.

136

ABILITIES

It is when nothing can be taken from us or offered to us that we have truly landed in a place where the path holds the most benefits.

In time you will notice your abilities changing. The further you walk the path and the more open you are, the more you will feel like your mind, body and soul are transforming. Life takes on a new perspective from the entirety of the life you have led before.

Life on the path is unlike any other and forces us to be and remain open to things we would never expect, nor would we have formerly listened to in our old lives.

When you are on the path, know that this is a

magical place where transformations occur. What transformations come with though is pain.

When a tree grows new roots, it is painful to push these roots into the ground. Some ground is soft and the mud is warm, allowing a tree to push its roots down and through easily. Some environments are extreme and ask trees to drive their roots into a ground that can barely even be called that as it is more like stepping onto concrete. What must be known about these two environments is that both are possible and impossible to live within.

Where the soft mud brings an easy opportunity to plant our roots, the concrete of a desert-like terrain seems impossible to push into. What we must remember is that living and surviving in both environments comes down to timing.

Where the soft mud is easy to push into, when there is too much rain a tree can fall over because the ground is not stable or solid enough to support it. The bigger the tree, the harder the tree will fall if the earth continues to be washed away with each oncoming rain.

Where the hard dirt of the desert appears to be too thick and hard for anything to break through, what we must wait for is the changing of seasons and the next burst of rain or dampness in the air. While this environment will not take a new seed every day, on the days where the ground is at its weakest and the Earth is cracked, a seed can fall into a crack and be taken in by the Earth.

Neither environment is easy and both will test your resolve and your ability to survive. Whether your foundation is soft and weak or you have grown up hard and able to survive in any environment, both will test you and both are a lot like the path.

What we must prepare for on the path is knowing that both environments exist and that we cannot expect every day to be easy, nor can we expect the path itself not to bring up challenges with our survival. Just because we have landed on the path, just as a seed lands on the ground in both environments, does not mean that we do not need to put in the work to plant our roots and continue to keep pushing day in and day out.

Landing yourself on the path, while it is an opportunity to find significant spiritual growth does not guarantee us abilities, nor does it ensure we will stay on or survive the path. However, if you can push through, plant your roots and continue to keep growing, you will notice that you have an ability to survive in any weather and in any environment.

You will notice that as you grow, your spiritual talents, abilities and staying power will grow too. There is a threshold we reach where so much has already been lost or shed on the path that nothing seems too much to lose anymore. It is when you reach this point on your travels that you will know you have made it and you will know that the path is yours forever.

Spend time on the path, remember the stories of both the muddy and the hard ground and know that both will require work from you daily to stay there. The biggest trees are often those who have grown and continued to grow through the most diversity. It is when we can grow in and through diversity that we will know true spiritual, physical and emotional freedom.

It is when we accept pain being part of the path that our wisdom will be felt through the ages, just as a tree's wisdom can be felt as generations come and go. If you are strong and if you are true in your intention, you will stay on the path no matter the weather, the challenges presented or what is offered to you to leave the path.

It is when nothing can be taken from us or offered to us that we have truly landed in a place where the path holds the most benefits. Your abilities as they develop will support you in this, giving you the magic to hold your ground and the ability to see the cracks in the hard earth where you can fall into and grow.

Life is about opportunity and timing. Ride with the timing when it supports you and stop when timing is bringing forth another solution. Trust yourself that you know the difference as we know you do. Just as we wait for the next season to come, so will you wait for the opportunity of when to run versus when to walk and so on.

Commit to the path like it is a lifelong partner and friend and it will treat you the same.

137

FLIGHT

When we allow ourselves to fly, we can see the bigger picture of our lives, how much we have changed and where we are heading.

There is a phrase in the sky that to be free; we must first fly.

When you are on the ground you cannot fly as the Earth does not give you the ability to see itself and the sky at once. To fly, you must first decide to leave the Earth, open your wings and shoot upwards.

To fly, you must know that you can launch and land again when the time is right and that leaving one place does not mean you are leaving it forever, you are only leaving it for a time.

When we allow ourselves to fly, we can see the

bigger picture of our lives, how much we have changed and where we are heading. When we are on the Earth, even when we find our way to the highest peaks, we still do not have the same visual abilities that we do in the sky. We are merely on Earth at the highest peak.

What the sky offers the Earth will never offer and vice versa. You will not find dirt in the sky, just as you will not find clouds on the ground. Both are separate and a connection to both is important for our spiritual development.

If you are smart you will seek both and allow both to touch, transform and mold your soul into something new. There are lessons to be learned from a life connected to both places and it is through a balance with the two that we will build both parts of ourselves at the same time.

Whereas someone connected to the Earth can read the signals of it through wildlife, weather, and nature, a person who is more connected to the sky can read what is not being seen or revealed on Earth as both hold a different connection and frequency. Just as Earth will never speak in the same way as the sky, the sky will never speak in the same way as Earth. Treat both like two different planets that make up a whole of the wisdom and insights you are learning to see.

Just as a river holds secrets for you beneath the surface of itself, on the riverbed, so does the inner lining of a cloud or the bird that flies within it or the lightning that moves through it.

Learn to read the signs of both the Earth and the sky and your learning and experience will take on a whole new meaning. Learn to see that one is not better or higher than the other and you will experience a balancing of elements that will support you on your journey, not hinder it.

And lastly, learn to see that your experience is different than that of others and that others can learn from you as much as you learn from them. What we each have is thousands of years of experience that has made us who we are today and each soul's set of experiences can help another soul to open their eyes to something new. Remember this when you meet someone who is struggling and remember that you do not need to be a spiritual teacher to have your love or your lessons felt by another.

It is through sharing that we grow and it is through

sharing that our roots can grow into a place far deeper than we ever imagined possible. The time we spend on the path sharing with others we meet is time invested in a way that promotes love, learning, and respect for all people who choose to walk a path that many others will turn away from. But do not spend all of your time on the path helping others as you will end up being a gatekeeper when all you wanted to do was become a guide. Where a gatekeeper guards the entrance, a guide walks the path and helps others walk with him or her along the way.

Be a student, be a guide, but leave the gatekeeping to us as this is not what you are here to do. We love you and support you always, in your dark times and in your light, when you are learning and when you feel stunted and unable to break free. Know that we are always with you and all you must do is ask for our help.

CHOICES

Life does not end when we have learned all of our lessons here on Earth, we then move to the sky and learn the ways of the universe, and we begin again in a new place.

The choices you make about your life affect who you are not just today and tomorrow, but also in future lifetimes and experiences to come.

At this point in your life you are blindly, but beautifully following a path that is uncertain, not guaranteed and for this we are grateful.

The lessons you have learned so far are bold and will someday be a very beautiful part of your path and also how you will feel when you eventually reach the destination.

When we speak of the destination, we ask that you know it may take many lifetimes to reach and even if we could describe it to you, no words will ever explain the beauty and freedom of what awaits you when the time is right and when all lessons here on Earth have been learned. We do not mean the lessons you are here to learn in this life, but all of your lessons over all of your lifetimes.

When all the fragmented pieces of your spirit have been put back together and all of your pain, loss, and trauma have been released and learned from. When everything you could ever have possibly wanted to know and learn about the Earth and yourself has been learned, over and over again and when the true self and true spirit has stepped forward, without masks and without a way of preparing itself for what it needs to do here.

It is when we are happy and ask to walk unprotected that we know you have learned that no pain, suffering or loss is so unbearable that you do not understand it or cannot walk through it.

It is when you are happy to embrace pain just as you embrace joy that we know you have come to appreciate both and all that it can offer you in insights into yourself and others. It is when we have come full circle and we know there is nothing left for us to take as all lessons have been taken that we will move onto a new path, in a new plane and existence.

Life does not end when we have learned all of our lessons here on Earth, we then move to the sky and learn the ways of the universe, and we begin again in a new place.

What this book has offered you is a chance and an opportunity to know and understand what the path will present to you before you have even entered it. Because as much as you feel you are on your way, the truth is, where you stand now is at the forefront and the beginning of the greatest adventure of your life.

What we promised you was a guide to the path and in this book contains the answers to anything and everything you will face and what everything always comes back to is moving forward regardless of what life on this planet throws at you on any given day.

It is removing yourself from the drama and illusions and seeing life here for what it really is, an opportunity to learn and to grow in a place where you have manifested as a human being that contains a spirit larger than the universe.

It is the journey of the spirit to be free, then to be housed by the body and the challenges that come with this only to realize that the body isn't a limitation, it's an opportunity to experience more. The body does not hold our spirit; the universe holds our spirit, the body is merely how we move around and gives us a face and a name to experience our time here.

If we can be bold in our choices and trust that whatever we experience we can move through it, with light, love, and intention we will find our way out of Earth and back to the sky once more.

In the final chapter, I will speak to you of what comes next as while there is a lifetime of learning in this book, the nature of a human being is to know which mountain is the next to conquer and climb. The path to enlightenment is only the beginning.

It is only by following the path that we will achieve moksha and it is only through moksha that we will be released to the universe again, like a star, a planet and a piece of dust.

The time we have on Earth, our time will be looked back upon fondly as one of the most testing experiences of our existence, but not one we would trade or swap for anything. Life on Earth is the greatest gift and the greatest spiritual burden we will experience, and still, we choose as spirits to come back and do it all over again.

We thank you for your kindness to yourself, to others and to us as we attempt to guide you into a space that your mind may not yet even be able to comprehend. Just know in time it will all begin to make sense, just as all of your experiences will make sense when you re-join us back in the sky.

We love you, we love your soul and the spirit to which you believe in life and what it offers both the energetic and the weary traveler.

Life on Earth is special, it is a gift and one that we do not wish to be taken away. Therefore, treat it like a gift, cherish it and seek to learn all you can from it, because the next chapter begins soon and when the time is right we will see you there and we will wait for you with open arms and an open heart.

139

THE END

What comes next for you dear traveller and the soul that lies within and around you is the lessons of the universe and universal law.

The light you have brought this world on your travels and in your existence in not just this life, but all of your lives are greater than any star in the sky and beyond the power and frequency that any star offers.

The journey you have traveled to reach this point has been one that has been earned over many lifetimes. Most do not step foot on this path until most lessons have been learned and we are seeking redemption and a reunion with our friends and family in the sky. Truth to be told, the sky has always been your home, it is when we venture to Earth and make the commitment to spend as long as we need there to learn our lessons that we may appreciate the freedom we have in the sky.

What comes next for you dear traveler and the soul that lies within and around you is the lessons of the universe and universal law.

While you may learn to operate within yourself and the world around you, the greater whole of life on Earth is learning our place within the universe and who and what is out there beyond our imagination and our wildest dreams. Learning who you are on Earth and how to ascend above it is just one hour in the age of the universe and discovering your place within the broader whole is what will allow you to fully embrace the beauty that is Earth and the experiences you have within it.

For a human being who does not understand life or pain, Earth can be a traumatic and unfruitful experience. Yet the further you travel along Earth's path, the more able you are to see, understand and experience what a life of pain and disharmony offers so that you may seek to find complete harmony and balance again. Finding harmony and balance on Earth means you have found harmony and balance within yourself, as a spirit and a soul that has come to this universe to learn.

What we will learn next are the ways of universal law and how knowing universal law can help you move more freely within your earthly surrounds.

It is through knowing the laws of the universe that we can see not only in the pain points in ourselves but in the world around us and Earth itself. It is by knowing the ways of the stars, the moon, Earth and everything that is encapsulated in our universe that we can see how tiny we are, but also how much change we can create for this planet if we know our place within the whole.

Life on Earth is a gift and the gift becomes even grander when we can appreciate and understand how limited our time is here and how Earth is not a permanent fixture in our universe. It is simply a star that was born that will one day die again when the universe deems its life to be over. The universe does not judge Earth for its crimes, it merely explains that just as life begins so will it end eventually and this is the same with the births and deaths of planets.

If you know in your heart that you wish to travel further and deeper into the universe, then we ask you to join us as we learn about the universe and what it has to offer us. It is by understanding universal law that we will fully know and understand our pain and also what we are trying to achieve here on Earth.

The path will not be easy and the lessons will not be easy, but where there is a will there is a way and if your soul is ready, you will join us. It is by knowing and treating the universe as our friend and with the respect it deserves that we will understand the fragility of our Earth and our place within it.

It is only by knowing how fragile and beautiful we are that we can appreciate why Earth is such a special and magical place. When we know this, we will stop abusing her and treating her as our playground, when we should treat her as our friend and mother. In time, you will understand what it means to be free in the universe, but first, you must free yourself.

Freedom is to be unchained in mind, thought, heart, body and spirit. Freedom is not needing to chain others or push ourselves and our ideas onto others. Not all will agree with these books, but those who are at a point in time where they are looking will find them and for them, the timing will be perfect.

Creating a serene Earth is what we have always desired and what our original gift was intended to be. Help us re-create a serene and giving Earth and you will help Earth renew in a universe that is as old as time itself. The universe existed before time and time is just a construct humans have created to define how long you have been here for. Truth be told, before you were here you were somewhere else and after you leave here, after all of your lessons have been learned and you offered mother Earth all you can, your soul and spirit will be transported to a new place, without memories of old. You will be a baby again in your mother's arms, eager to grow, learn and transform. When you reach this place and time, you will know you will have come full circle, but you will not remember this.

We love you, and we appreciate your time, your effort and your faith that the smallest of actions can create the largest ripples in the universe. Time is not how we keep track of who you are and what you have made, time is merely a way of knowing that you existed at all.

What we cherish and love about humanity is when you act from a place of love, selflessness and when you work to enhance the life and love of others. This is what you have come here to learn. Life on Earth is not about you and what you wish to achieve, it is a life and lives of service offered back to the mother who created you. Learn this and you will be free.

For Those Who Have Woken

Thank you for reading.

If you enjoyed Awakened Souls please stay tuned for my next book, Universal Law. Or go back and read my first channeled book, Conversations with Krishna.

To stay in touch, visit www.courtneybeck.co for one-on-one healing sessions, spiritual mentoring or download a healing meditation infused with the energies of my spirit guides.

www.ingramcontent.com/pod-product-compliance
Lightning Source LLC
Chambersburg PA
CBHW020312010526
44107CB00054B/1814